BASIC  PROBABILITY

What Every Math Student Should Know

BASIC
PROBABILITY
What Every Math Student
Should Know

Henk Tijms

 **World Scientific**

NEW JERSEY · LONDON · SINGAPORE · BEIJING · SHANGHAI · HONG KONG · TAIPEI · CHENNAI · TOKYO

Published by

World Scientific Publishing Co. Pte. Ltd.

5 Toh Tuck Link, Singapore 596224

USA office: 27 Warren Street, Suite 401-402, Hackensack, NJ 07601

UK office: 57 Shelton Street, Covent Garden, London WC2H 9HE

Library of Congress Cataloging-in-Publication Data

Names: Tijms, H. C., author.

Title: Basic probability : what every math student should know / by
Henk Tijms (Vrije University, The Netherlands).

Description: New Jersey : World Scientific, 2019. | Includes index.

Identifiers: LCCN 2019011641| ISBN 9789811202353 (hardcover : alk. paper) |
ISBN 9789811203763 (pbk. : alk. paper)

Subjects: LCSH: Probabilities--Textbooks.

Classification: LCC QA273.2 .T54 2019 | DDC 519.2--dc23

LC record available at https://lccn.loc.gov/2019011641

British Library Cataloguing-in-Publication Data

A catalogue record for this book is available from the British Library.

For any available supplementary material, please visit
https://www.worldscientific.com/worldscibooks/10.1142/11334#t=suppl

Printed in Singapore

Preface

Probability is a fascinating branch of mathematics that is indispensable to statistical literacy and basic logical thinking. In modern society it is necessary to be able to analyze probability claims in the media and to make informed judgments and decisions. This book provides a basic knowledge of probability theory and reasoning, and illustrates it with many colorful everyday situations involving uncertainty.

This book is written for high school and college students learning about probability for the first time. Though it is a very short introduction to probability, the book covers all the essential aspects that every math and statistics student should know. A short book like this one is particularly suitable for courses that struggle with managing time to cover the basics of probability. Key features of the book are conditional probability and Bayesian probability, striking applications of the Poisson distribution, and the interface between probability and computer simulation. The emphasis is on discrete probability, but attention is also given to the important normal distribution and the celebrated central limit theorem. Scattered throughout the text, many remarks are made on the history of probability.

Problems and problem-solving are very important in probability. Each chapter contains insightful examples and instructive problems. Answers to most problems and fully worked-out solutions to selected problems are provided to stimulate the students' active learning.

Contents

Chapter 4. Surprising World of Poisson Probabilities   79

Chapter 5. Computer Simulation and Probability   89

Solutions to Selected Problems   111

Chapter 1

Combinatorics and Calculus for Probability

This chapter presents a number of results from combinatorics and calculus, in preparation for the subsequent chapters. Section 1.1 introduces you to the concepts of factorials and binomial coefficients. In section 1.2 the exponential function and the natural logarithm will be discussed.

1.1 Factorials and binomial coefficients

Many probability problems require counting techniques. In particular, these techniques are extremely useful for computing probabilities in a chance experiment in which all possible outcomes are equally likely. In such experiments, one needs effective methods to count the number of outcomes in any specific event. In counting problems, it is important to know whether the order in which the elements are counted is relevant or not. Factorials and binomial coefficients will be discussed and illustrated.

In the discussion below, the fundamental principle of counting is frequently used: if there are a ways to do one activity and b ways to do another activity, then there are $a \times b$ ways of doing both. As an example, suppose that you go to a restaurant to get some breakfast. The menu says pancakes, waffles, or fried eggs, while for a drink you can choose between juice, coffee, tea, and hot chocolate. Then the total number of different choices of food and drink is $3 \times 4 = 12$. As another example, how many different license plates are possible when the license plate displays a nonzero digit, followed by three letters, followed by three digits? The answer is $9 \times 26 \times 26 \times 26 \times 10 \times 10 \times 10 =$ 158 184 000 license plates.

Factorials and permutations

How many different ways can you order a number of different objects such as letters or numbers? For example, what is the number of different ways that the three letters A, B, and C can be ordered? By writing out all the possibilities ABC, ACB, BAC, BCA, CAB, and CBA, you can see that the total number is 6. This brute-force method of writing down all the possibilities and counting them is naturally not practical when the number of possibilities gets large, as is the case for the number of possible orderings of the 26 letters of the alphabet. You can also determine that the three letters A, B, and C can be ordered in 6 different ways by reasoning as follows. For the first position, there are 3 available letters to choose from, for the second position there are 2 letters over to choose from, and only one letter for the third position. Therefore the total number of possibilities is $3 \times 2 \times 1 = 6$. The general rule should now be evident. Suppose that you have n distinguishable objects. How many ordered arrangements of these objects are possible? Any ordered sequence of the objects is called a *permutation*. Reasoning similar to that described shows that there are n ways for choosing the first object, leaving $n - 1$ choices for the second object, etc. Therefore the total number of ways to order n distinguishable objects is $n \times (n - 1) \times \cdots \times 2 \times 1$. This product is denoted by $n!$ and is called 'n factorial'. Thus, for any positive integer n,

$$n! = 1 \times 2 \times \cdots \times (n - 1) \times n.$$

A useful convention is

$$0! = 1,$$

which simplifies the presentation of several formulas to be given below. Note that $n! = n \times (n - 1)!$ and so $n!$ grows very quickly as n gets larger. For example, $5! = 720$, $10! = 3\,628\,800$ and $15! = 1\,307\,674\,368\,000$. Summarizing, for any positive integer n,

the total number of ordered sequences (permutations) of n distinguishable objects is $n!$.

Armed with this knowledge, you are asked to argue that in the lottery 6/45 the six lotto numbers, which are drawn one by one from 1 to 45, will appear in either an ascending or descending order with a probability of $\frac{1}{360}$.

An interesting question is how may different words, whether or not existing, can be constructed from a given number of letters where some letters appear multiple times. For example, how many different words can be constructed from five letters A, two letters B, two letters R, one letter C, and one letter D? To answer this question, imagine that the five letters A are numbered as A_1 to A_5, the two letters B as B_1 and B_2, and the two letters R as R_1 and R_2. Then you have 11 different letters and the number of ways to order those letters is 11!. The five letters A_1 to A_5, the two letters B_1 and B_2, and the two letters R_1 and R_2 can among themselves be ordered in $5! \times 2! \times 2!$ ways. Each of these orderings gives the same word if you replace A_1 to A_5 by A, B_1 and B_2 by B, and R_1 and R_2 by R. Thus the total number of different words that can be formed from the original 11 letters is

$$\frac{11!}{5! \times 2! \times 2!} = 83\,160.$$

Thus, if you thoroughly mix the eleven letters and then put them in a row, the probability of getting the word ABRACADABRA is $\frac{1}{83\,160}$.

Binomial coefficients and combinations

How many different juries of three persons can be formed from five persons A, B, C, D, and E? By direct enumeration you see that the answer is 10: $\{A, B, C\}$, $\{A, B, D\}$, $\{A, B, E\}$, $\{A, C, D\}$, $\{A, C, E\}$, $\{A, D, E\}$, $\{B, C, D\}$, $\{B, C, E\}$, $\{B, D, E\}$, and $\{C, D, E\}$. In this problem, the order in which the jury members are chosen is not relevant. The answer 10 juries could also have been obtained by a basic principle of counting. First, count how many juries of three persons are possible when attention is paid to the order. Then determine how often each group of three persons has been counted. Thus the reasoning is as follows. There are 5 ways to select the first jury member, 4 ways to then select the next member, and 3 ways to select the final member. This would give $5 \times 4 \times 3$ ways of forming the jury when the order in which the members are chosen would be relevant. However, this order makes no difference. For example, for the jury consisting of the persons A, B and C, it is not relevant which of the $3!$ ordered sequences ABC, ACB, BAC, BCA, CAB, and CBA has lead to the jury. Hence the total number of ways a jury of 3 persons can be formed from a group of 5 persons is equal to $\frac{5 \times 4 \times 3}{3!}$. This expression can be rewritten as

$$\frac{5 \times 4 \times 3 \times 2 \times 1}{3! \times 2!} = \frac{5!}{3! \times 2!}.$$

In general, you can calculate that the total number of possible ways to choose a jury of k persons out of a group of n persons is equal to

$$\frac{n \times (n-1) \times \cdots \times (n-k+1)}{k!}$$
$$= \frac{n \times \cdots \times (n-k+1) \times (n-k) \times \cdots \times 1}{k! \times (n-k)!} = \frac{n!}{k! \times (n-k)!}.$$

This leads to the definition

$$\binom{n}{k} = \frac{n!}{k! \times (n-k)!}$$

for nonnegative integers n and k with $k \leq n$. The quantity $\binom{n}{k}$ (pronounce: n over k) has the interpretation:

$\binom{n}{k}$ **is the total number of ways to choose k different objects out of n distinguishable objects, paying no attention to their order.**

In other words, $\binom{n}{k}$ is the total number of combinations of k different objects out of n and is referred to as the *binomial coefficient*. The key difference between permutations and combinations is *order*. Combinations are *unordered* selections, permutations are *ordered* arrangements.

The binomial coefficients play a key role in the so-called *urn model*. This model has many applications in probability. Suppose that an urn contains R red and W white balls. What is the probability of getting exactly r red balls when blindly grasping n balls from the urn? To answer this question, it is helpful to imagine that the balls are made distinguishable by giving each of them a different label. The total number of possible combinations of n different balls is $\binom{R+W}{n}$. Under these combinations there are $\binom{R}{r} \times \binom{W}{n-r}$ combinations with exactly r red balls (and thus $n - r$ white balls). Thus, if you blindly grasp n balls from the urn, the probability of getting exactly r red balls is given by

$$\frac{\binom{R}{r} \times \binom{W}{n-r}}{\binom{R+W}{n}}$$

with the convention that $\binom{a}{b} = 0$ for $b > a$. These probabilities represent the so-called *hypergeometric distribution*. Probability problems that can be translated into the urn model appear in many disguises. A nice illustration is the lotto 6/45. In each drawing six different numbers are chosen from the numbers $1, 2, \ldots, 45$. Suppose you have filled in one ticket with six numbers. Then the probability of matching exactly r of the six numbers drawn is

$$\frac{\binom{6}{r} \times \binom{39}{6-r}}{\binom{45}{6}} \qquad \text{for } r = 0, 1, \ldots, 6,$$

as you can see by identifying the six drawn numbers with 6 red balls and the other 39 numbers with 39 white balls. In particular, the probability of matching all 6 numbers drawn (the jackpot) is 1 to $8\,145\,060$.

In mathematics there are many identities in which binomial coefficients appear. The following recursive relation is known as Pascal's triangle[1]:

$$\binom{n}{k} = \binom{n-1}{k-1} + \binom{n-1}{k} \qquad \text{for } 1 \le k \le n.$$

---

[1] Pascal was far from the first to study this triangle. The Persian mathematician Al-Karaji had produced something very similar as early as the 10th century, and the triangle is called Yang Hui's triangle in China after the 13th century Chinese mathematician, and Tartaglia's triangle in Italy after the 16th century Italian mathematician Niccolò Tartaglia.

You can algebraically prove this. A more elegant proof is by interpreting the same 'thing' in two different ways. This is called a word-proof. Think of a group of n persons from which a committee of k persons must be chosen. The k persons can be chosen in $\binom{n}{k}$ ways. However, you can also count as follows. Take a particular person, say John. The number of possible committees containing John is $\binom{n-1}{k-1}$ and the number of possible committees not containing John is $\binom{n-1}{k}$, which verifies the identity.

Try yourselves the following test questions:

• How many distinct license plates with three letters followed by three digits are possible? How many if the letters and numbers must be different? (answer: $17\,576\,000$ and $11\,232\,000$)

• What is the number of ways to arrange 5 letters A and 3 letters B in a row? (answer: 56)

• Five football players A, B, C, D and E are designated to take a penalty kick after the end of a football match. In how many orders can they shoot if A must shoot immediately after C? How many if A must shoot after C? (answer: 24 and 60)

• What is the total number of distinguishable permutations of the eleven letters in the word Mississippi? (answer: $34\,650$)

• A group of people consists of five persons of the Dutch nationality and five persons of the British nationality. In how many ways, five persons can be chosen with the restriction that exactly three persons of the British nationality must be included? (answer: 100)

• John and Pete are among 10 players who are to be divided into two teams of five. How many formations of the teams are possible so that John and Pete belong to a same team? (answer: 112)

• Suppose that from 10 children, five are to be chosen and lined up. How many different lines are possible? (answer: $30\,240$)

• Give word proofs of $\binom{n}{n-k} = \binom{n}{k}$ and $\sum_{k=0}^{n} \binom{n}{k}\binom{n}{n-k} = \binom{2n}{n}$.

1.2 Basic results from calculus

The Euler number e, the exponential function and the natural logarithm are often used in probability. This section discusses these mathematical basic concepts. Also, some results for the geometric and harmonic series are given.

Exponential function

The history of the number e begins with the discovery of logarithms by John Napier in 1614. At this time in history, international trade was experiencing a period of strong growth, and, as a result, there was much attention given to the concept of compound interest. At that time, it was already noticed that $(1 + \frac{1}{n})^n$ tends to a certain limit if n is allowed to increase without bound:

$$\lim_{n \to \infty} \left(1 + \frac{1}{n}\right)^n = e,$$

where

$$e = 2.7182818\ldots.$$

The famous mathematical constant e is called the Euler number. This constant is named after Leonhard Euler (1707–1783) who is considered as the most productive mathematician in history.

The *exponential function* is defined by e^x, where the variable x runs through the real numbers. This is one of the most important functions in mathematics. A fundamental property of e^x is that this function has itself as derivative:

$$\frac{de^x}{dx} = e^x \quad \text{for all } x.$$

Intermezzo: Let's give a simple argument. Consider a function $a(x)$ of the specific form $a(x) = a^x$ for some constant $a > 0$. Then, for each $h > 0$,

$$\frac{a(x+h) - a(x)}{h} = \frac{a^{x+h} - a^x}{h} = a(x)\frac{a^h - 1}{h}.$$

Take for granted that $c = \lim_{h \to 0}(a^h - 1)/h$ exists. Thus $a'(x) = ca(x)$. When is the constant $c = 1$? The answer is if $a = e$. To see this, note that the condition $\lim_{h \to 0}(a^h - 1)/h = 1$ is the same as $a = \lim_{h \to 0}(1 + h)^{1/h} =$

$\lim_{n\to\infty}(1+\frac{1}{n})^n = e$. This shows that $a'(x) = a(x)$ if $a = e$. A more general result is that $f(x) = e^x$ is the only function satisfying the differential equation $f'(x) = f(x)$ with the boundary condition $f(0) = 1$.

How to calculate the function e^x? The generally valid relation

$$\lim_{n\to\infty}\left(1 + \frac{x}{n}\right)^n = e^x \quad \text{for all } x$$

is not useful for that purpose. The calculation of e^x is based on the power series

$$e^x = 1 + x + \frac{x^2}{2!} + \frac{x^3}{3!} + \cdots \quad \text{for all } x.$$

The proof of this power series expansion requires Taylor's theorem from calculus. The fact that e^x has itself as derivative is crucial in the proof. Note that term-by-term differentiation of the series $1 + x + \frac{x^2}{2!} + \cdots$ leads to the same series, in agreement with the fact that e^x has itself as derivative. The series expansion of e^x leads to the accurate approximation formula

$$e^x \approx 1 + x \quad \text{for } x \text{ close to } 0.$$

This is one of the most useful approximation formulas in mathematics! In probability theory the formula is often used in the alternative form

$$1 - e^{-\lambda} \approx \lambda \quad \text{for } \lambda \text{ close to } 0.$$

A nice illustration of the usefulness of this formula is provided by the birthday problem. What is the probability that two or more people share a birthday in a randomly formed group of m people (no twins)? To simplify the analysis, it is assumed that the year has 365 days (February 29 is excluded) and that each of these days is equally likely as birthday. Number the people as 1 to m en let the sequence $(v_1, v_2, \ldots, v_m)$ denote their birthdays. The total number of possible sequences is $365 \times 365 \times \cdots \times 365 = 365^m$, while the number of sequences in which each person has a different birthday is $365 \times 364 \times \cdots \times (365 - m + 1)$. Denoting by P_m the probability that each person has a different birthday, you have

$$P_m = \left[365 \times 364 \times \cdots \times (365 - m + 1)\right]/365^m.$$

If m is much smaller than 365, the insightful approximation

$$P_m \approx e^{-\frac{1}{2}m(m-1)/365}$$

applies. To see this, write P_m as

$$P_m = 1 \times \left(1 - \frac{1}{365}\right) \times \left(1 - \frac{2}{365}\right) \times \cdots \times \left(1 - \frac{m-1}{365}\right).$$

Next, using the approximation $e^{-x} \approx 1 - x$ for x close to zero and the well-known algebraic formula $1 + 2 + \cdots + n = \frac{1}{2}n(n+1)$ for $n \geq 1$, you get

$$P_m \approx e^{-1/365} \times e^{-2/365} \times \cdots \times e^{-(m-1)/365} = e^{-(1+2+\ldots+m-1)/365}$$

$$= e^{-\frac{1}{2}m(m-1)/365}.$$

The sought probability that two or more people share a same birthday is one minus the probability that each person has a different birthday and can thus be approximated by $1 - e^{-\frac{1}{2}m(m-1)/365}$. This probability is already more than 50% for $m = 23$ people (the exact value is 0.5073 and the approximate value is 0.5000). The intuitive explanation that the probability of a match is already more than 50% for such a small value of $m = 23$ is that there are $\binom{23}{2} = 253$ combinations of two persons, each combination having a matching probability of $\frac{1}{365}$.

Natural logarithm

The function e^x is strictly increasing on $(-\infty, \infty)$ with $\lim_{x \to -\infty} e^x = 0$ and $\lim_{x \to \infty} e^x = \infty$. As a consequence, the equation $e^y = c$ has a unique solution y for each $c > 0$. This solution as function of c is called the *natural logarithm* and is denoted by $\ln(c)$ for $c > 0$. Thus the natural logarithm is the inverse function of the exponential function. In other words, $\ln(x)$ is the logarithmic function with base e. The natural logarithm can also be defined by the integral

$$\ln(y) = \int_1^y \frac{1}{v} \, dv \quad \text{for } y > 0.$$

This integral representation of $\ln(y)$, which is often used in probability analysis, shows that $\ln(y)$ has $\frac{1}{y}$ as derivative for $y > 0$.

Geometric and harmonic series

In probability analysis you will often encounter the geometric series. The basic formula for the geometric series is

$$1 + x + x^2 + \cdots = \frac{1}{1-x} \quad \text{for } |x| < 1,$$

or, shortly, $\sum_{k=0}^{\infty} x^k = \frac{1}{1-x}$ for $|x| < 1$. You can easily verify this result by working out $(1-x)(1+x+x^2+\cdots+x^m)$ as $1 - x^{m+1}$. If you take $|x| < 1$ and you let m tend to infinity, then x^{m+1} tends to 0. This gives $(1-x)(1+x+x^2+\cdots) = 1$ for $|x| < 1$, which verifies the desired result. Differentiating the geometric series term for term and noting that $\frac{1}{1-x}$ has $\frac{1}{(1-x)^2}$ as derivative, you get another useful formula:

$$1 + 2x + 3x^2 + \cdots = \frac{1}{(1-x)^2} \quad \text{for } |x| < 1.$$

or, shortly, $\sum_{k=1}^{\infty} kx^{k-1} = \frac{1}{(1-x)^2}$ for $|x| < 1$. The formulas for the geometric series are very useful in probability.

The partial sum $1 + \frac{1}{2} + \cdots + \frac{1}{n}$ of the harmonic series appears in the solutions of a variety of probability problems. An insightful approximation is

$$1 + \frac{1}{2} + \cdots + \frac{1}{n} \approx \ln(n) + \gamma + \frac{1}{2n} \quad \text{for } n \text{ large,}$$

where $\gamma = 0.57721566\ldots$ is the Euler-Mascheroni constant. The approximation is very accurate and can be explained from the integral representation for $\ln(y)$. It is interesting to note that the partial sum $\sum_{k=1}^{n} \frac{1}{k}$ increases extremely slowly as n gets larger.[2] To illustrate this, the number of terms needed to exceed the sum 100 is about 1.509×10^{43} and the number of terms needed to exceed the sum 1,000 is about 1.106×10^{434}.

---

[2]The harmonic series $\sum_{k=1}^{\infty} \frac{1}{k}$ diverges and has the value ∞. There are many proofs for this celebrated result. The first proof dates back to about 1350 and was given by the philosopher Nicolas Oresme. His argument was ingenious. Oresme simply observed that $\frac{1}{3} + \frac{1}{4} > \frac{2}{4} = \frac{1}{2}$, $\frac{1}{5} + \frac{1}{6} + \frac{1}{7} + \frac{1}{8} > \frac{4}{8} = \frac{1}{2}$, $\frac{1}{9} + \frac{1}{10} + \cdots + \frac{1}{16} > \frac{8}{16} = \frac{1}{2}$, etc. In general, $\frac{1}{r+1} + \frac{1}{r+2} + \cdots + \frac{1}{2r} > \frac{1}{2}$ for any r, showing that $\sum_{k=1}^{n} \frac{1}{k}$ eventually grows beyond any bound as n gets larger. Isn't it a beautiful argument?

Appendix: Poisson distribution as limit of the binomial distribution

This appendix shows how the formula $e^x = \lim_{n \to \infty} \left(1 + \frac{x}{n}\right)^n$ can be used to relate the Poisson and binomial distributions. These distributions are the subject of section 3.1. For any positive integer n and number p between 0 and 1, let

$$b_k = \binom{n}{k} p^k (1-p)^{n-k} \quad \text{for } k = 0, 1, \ldots, n.$$

The b_k's represent the so-called binomial distribution with parameters n and p. If n tends to infinity and p to zero such that np tends to a constant $\lambda > 0$, then b_k converges to

$$p_k = e^{-\lambda} \frac{\lambda^k}{k!} \quad \text{for } k = 0, 1, \ldots .$$

The p_k's represent the so-called Poisson distribution with parameter λ. To avoid technicalities, the limiting result is only proved for the case that np is kept fixed on the value λ $(p = \frac{\lambda}{n})$. The proof then goes as follows: write $\binom{n}{k} p^k (1-p)^{n-k}$ as

$$\binom{n}{k} \left(\frac{\lambda}{n}\right)^k \left(1 - \frac{\lambda}{n}\right)^{n-k} = \frac{n!}{k!\,(n-k)!} \frac{\lambda^k}{n^k} \frac{(1 - \lambda/n)^n}{(1 - \lambda/n)^k}$$

$$= \frac{\lambda^k}{k!} \left(1 - \frac{\lambda}{n}\right)^n \left[\frac{n!}{n^k\,(n-k)!}\right] \left(1 - \frac{\lambda}{n}\right)^{-k}.$$

The next step in the proof is to fix k and to analyze separately the terms in the last expression. The first term $\frac{\lambda^k}{k!}$ is left untouched. The second term $\left(1 - \frac{\lambda}{n}\right)^n$ tends to $e^{-\lambda}$ if n tends to infinity. The third term can be written as:

$$\frac{n!}{n^k\,(n-k)!} = \frac{n(n-1)\cdots(n-k+1)}{n^k}$$

$$= \left(1 - \frac{1}{n}\right)\left(1 - \frac{2}{n}\right)\cdots\left(1 - \frac{k-1}{n}\right).$$

Thus, for fixed k, the third term tends to 1 if n tends to infinity. For fixed k, the last term $\left(1 - \frac{\lambda}{n}\right)^{-k}$ also tends to 1 if n tends to infinity. This completes the proof.

To conclude this appendix, the following two formulas for Poisson probabilities are stated:

$$\sum_{k=0}^{\infty} k e^{-\lambda} \frac{\lambda^k}{k!} = \lambda \quad \text{and} \quad \sum_{k=0}^{\infty} k(k-1) e^{-\lambda} \frac{\lambda^k}{k!} = \lambda^2.$$

It is a matter of simple algebraic manipulations to get these formulas, which will be used in section 3.1. Noting that $k! = k \times (k-1)!$, it follows that

$$\sum_{k=0}^{\infty} k e^{-\lambda} \frac{\lambda^k}{k!} = \lambda e^{-\lambda} \sum_{k=1}^{\infty} \frac{\lambda^{k-1}}{(k-1)!} = \lambda e^{-\lambda} \sum_{j=0}^{\infty} \frac{\lambda^j}{j!} = \lambda e^{-\lambda} e^{\lambda} = \lambda,$$

using the fact that $e^x = \sum_{j=0}^{\infty} \frac{x^j}{j!}$. In the same way, you can obtain the other formula.

Chapter 2
Basics of Elementary Probability

The goal of this chapter is to familiarize you with the most important basic concepts and results in elementary probability. The probability model and the axioms are first discussed. Then the essentials of conditional probability and Bayesian probability are covered. Thereafter the concepts of random variable, expected value and standard deviation are introduced. All this is illustrated with insightful examples and instructive problems.

2.1 Foundation of probability

Approximately four hundred years after colorful Italian mathematician and physician Gerolamo Cardano (1501–1576) wrote his book *Liber de Ludo Aleae* (The Book of Games of Chance) and laid a cornerstone for the foundation of the field of probability by introducing the concept of *sample space*, celebrated Russian mathematician Andrey Kolmogorov (1903–1987) cemented that foundation with axioms on which a solid theory can be built.

The sample space of a chance experiment is a set of elements that one-to-one correspond to all of the possible outcomes of that experiment. To illustrate, the sample space of the experiment of rolling a die once can be taken as the finite set of the numbers 1 to 6, the sample space of the experiment of rolling a die until a six appears can be taken as the countably infinite set of the positive integers, and the sample space of the experiment of measuring the time until the first emission from a radioactive source can be taken as the uncountable set of the positive real numbers.

The idea of Kolmogorov was to consider a sufficiently rich class of subsets of the sample space and to assign a number, $P(A)$, between 0 and 1, to each subset A belonging to this class of subsets. The class of subsets consists of all possible subsets if the sample space is finite or countably infinite, but certain 'weird' subsets must be excluded if the sample space is uncountable. For the probability measure P, three natural postulates are assumed. Denoting by $P(A$ or $B)$ the number assigned to the set of all outcomes belonging to either subset A or subset B or to both, the axioms for a finite sample space are:

Axiom 1. $P(\Omega) = 1$ *for the sample space* Ω.

Axiom 2. $0 \leq P(A) \leq 1$ *for each subset A of* Ω.

Axiom 3. $P(A$ or $B) = P(A) + P(B)$ *if the subsets A and B have no element in common (so-called disjoint subsets).*

The third axiom requires a minor modification in the case of a non-finite sample space. The sample space endowed with a probability measure P on the class of subsets is called a *probability space*.

If the sample space contains a countable number of elements, it is sufficient to assign a probability $p(\omega)$ to each element ω of the sample space. The probability $P(A)$ that is then assigned to a subset A of the sample space is defined by the sum of the probabilities of the individual elements of set A. That is, in mathematical notation,

$$P(A) = \sum_{\omega \in A} p(\omega).$$

A special case is the case of a finite sample space in which each outcome is equally likely. Then $P(A)$ can be calculated as

$$P(A) = \frac{\text{the number of outcomes belonging to } A}{\text{the total number of outcomes of the sample space}}.$$

This probability model is known as the *Laplace model,* named after the famous French scientist Pierre Simon Laplace (1749–1827), who is sometimes called the 'French Newton'. What is called the Laplace model was first introduced by Gerolamo Cardano in his 16th century book. This probability model was used to solve a main problem in early probability: the probability of not getting a 1 in two rolls of a fair die is $\frac{25}{36}$. Galileo Galilei (1564–1642), one of the greatest scientists of the Renaissance, used the model to explain to the Grand Duke of Toscany, his benefactor, that it is more likely to get a sum of 10 than a sum of 11 in a single roll of three fair dice (the probabilities are $\frac{27}{216}$ and $\frac{25}{216}$).

In probability language, any subset A of the sample space is called an *event*. It is said that event A occurs if the outcome of the experiment belongs to the set A. The number $P(A)$ is the probability that event A will occur. Any individual outcome is also an event, but events correspond typically to more than one outcome. For example, the sample space of the experiment of a single roll of a die is the set $\{1, 2, 3, 4, 5, 6\}$, where outcome i means that i dots appear on the up face of the die. Then, the subset $A = \{1, 3, 5\}$ represents the event that the die lands on an odd number. Events A and B are called *disjoint* (or *mutually exclusive*) if the sets A and B are disjoint.

The probability measure P does not appear out of thin air, rather you must consciously choose it. Naturally, this must be done in such a way that the axioms are satisfied and the model reflects the reality of the problem at hand in the best possible way. The axioms must hold true not only for the interpretation of probabilities in terms of the relative frequencies for a repeatable experiment such as the rolling of a die. They must also remain valid for the Bayesian interpretation of probability as a measure of personal belief in the outcome of a non-repeatable probability experiment, such as, for example, a horse race.

Example 2.1. What is the probability that the largest number rolled in a single roll of two fair dice is 4?

Solution. The line of thought is made easier if you imagine that one die is blue, and the other is red. The set consisting of the 36 outcomes (i, j) with $i, j = 1, 2, \ldots, 6$ is taken as sample space for the experiment, where i represents the number of points rolled with the blue die, and j represents the number of points rolled with the red die. The dice are fair so that an appropriate probability model is constructed by assigning the same probability $\frac{1}{36}$ to each element of the sample space. This model is an instance of the Laplace model: in order to find the probability of an event, you count the number of favorable outcomes and divide them by the total number of possible outcomes. Let A be the event that the largest number rolled is 4. The event A occurs only if the experiment gives one of the seven outcomes $(1,4)$, $(2,4)$, $(3,4)$, $(4,4)$, $(4,3)$, $(4,2)$ and $(4,1)$. Thus $P(A) = \frac{7}{36}$, or,

$$P(\text{the largest number in the roll of the two dice is 4}) = \frac{7}{36}.$$

Sample points may be easily incorrectly counted. In his book *Opera Omnia* the German mathematician Gottfried Wilhelm Leibniz (1646–1716) – inventor of differential and integral calculus along with Isaac Newton – made a famous mistake by stating: "with two dice, it is equally likely to roll twelve points than to roll eleven points, because one or the other can be done in only one manner". He argued: two sixes for a sum 12, and a five and a six for a sum 11. However, there are two ways to get a sum 11, as is obvious by imagining that one die is blue and the other is red. Alternatively, you may think of two rolls of a single die rather than a single roll of two dice.

Example 2.2. Two desperados, A and B, are playing a game of Russian roulette, using a pistol. One of the pistol's six cylinders contains a bullet. The desperados take turns pointing the gun at their own heads and pulling the trigger. Desperado A begins. If no fatal shot is fired, they give the cylinder a spin such that it stops at a random chamber, and the round continues with desperado B. What is the probability that desperado A will fire the fatal shot?

Solution. The set $\{1, 2, \ldots\}$ of the positive integers is taken as sample space for the experiment. Outcome i means that the fatal shot occurs at the ith trial. An appropriate probability model is constructed by assigning the probability $\frac{1}{6}$ to outcome 1, the probability $\frac{5}{6} \times \frac{1}{6}$ to outcome 2, and, the probability p_i to outcome i, where

$$p_i = \frac{5}{6} \times \cdots \times \frac{5}{6} \times \frac{1}{6} = \left(\frac{5}{6}\right)^{i-1} \times \frac{1}{6} \quad \text{for } i = 1, 2, \ldots.$$

Let A be the event that desperado A fires the fatal shot. This event occurs for the outcomes $1, 3, 5, \ldots$. Thus $P(A) = \sum_{k=0}^{\infty} p_{2k+1} = \frac{1}{6} \sum_{k=0}^{\infty} (\frac{25}{36})^k$. Using the geometric series $\sum_{k=0}^{\infty} x^k = \frac{1}{1-x}$ for $|x| < 1$, you get

$$P(\text{desperado A will fire the fatal shot}) = \frac{1}{6} \times \frac{1}{1 - 25/36} = \frac{6}{11}.$$

In Example 2.2 the so-called *geometric probability model* was used: a sequence of physically independent trials each having the same probability p of success is performed until a success occurs for the first time (physical independence means that the result of one trial does not affect the result of any other trial). In this useful model, the probability $(1 - p)^{i-1} p$ is assigned to the event that the first success occurs at the ith trial for $i = 1, 2, \ldots$.

It is fun to give also a probability problem with an uncountable sample space. The problem is a geometric probability problem.

Example 2.3. The game of franc-carreau was a popular game in 18th-century France. In this game, a coin is tossed on a chessboard. The player wins if the coin does not fall on one of the lines of the board. Suppose now that a round coin with a diameter of d is blindly tossed on a large table. The surface of the table is divided into squares whose sides measure a in length, such that $a > d$. What is the probability of the coin falling entirely within the confines of a square?

Solution. The trick is to concentrate on the center point of the coin. Take as sample space the square in which this point falls. The meaning of a point in the sample space is that the center of the coin lands on that point. Since the coin lands randomly on the table, the probability that is assigned to each neat subset A of the sample space is the area of the region A divided by the area of the square. The coin falls entirely within the confines of the square if and only if the center point of the coin lands on a point in the shaded square in Figure 1. The area of the shaded square is $(a - d)^2$. Therefore

$$P(\text{the coin will fall entirely within a square}) = \frac{(a - d)^2}{a^2}.$$

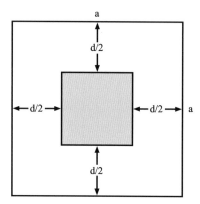

Figure 1: Franc-carreau game

Complement rule

One of the most useful calculation rules in the field of probability is the complement rule, which states that the probability of a given event occurring can be found by calculating the probability that the event will not occur. These two probabilities sum to 1. The complement rule is often used to find the probability of 'something' occurring at least once. For example, the rule is very helpful to find the probability of at least one six occurring in four rolls of a die and the probability of at least one double six in 24 rolls of two dice, see Problem 2.2 below. This probability problem has an interesting history. The French nobleman Chevalier de Méré was a famous gambler of the 17th century. He frequently offered the bet that he could obtain a six in four rolls or less of a single die and the bet that he could obtain a double six with two dice in 24 rolls or less. The Chevalier believed that the chance of winning the bet was the same in both games (can you explain why the respective chances are not $\frac{4}{6}$ and $\frac{24}{36}$?). In reality, however, he won the first game more often than not, but, to his big surprise, he lost the second game more often than not. The Chevalier approached the mathematician Blaise Pascal for clarification. This inquiry led to a correspondence between the two famous French mathematicians Blaise Pascal (1623–1662) and Pierre de Fermat (1601–1665).[3] They mathematically clarified the dice problem by simply calculating the chances of *not* rolling a six or double six.

The complement rule is discussed in more detail in the next example. This example is a variant of the birthday problem in section 1.2.

Example 2.4. The game of European roulette is played on a roulette wheel containing 37 slots numbered from $0, 1, 2, \ldots, 36$. In each round of the game, every slot has the same probability of being the one where the roulette ball lands. What is the probability that, during the next 7 rounds of the game, the ball will land in a same slot two or more times?

Solution. Take the set of all possible sequences $(i_1, i_2, \ldots, i_7)$ as sample space, whereby i_k is the number of the slot in which the ball lands in the kth round. The sample space has $37 \times 37 \times \cdots \times 37 = 37^7$ equally likely outcomes. Let A be the event that the ball lands in one of the slots two or more times. Rather than calculating the probability $P(A)$, it is simpler to calculate the complementary probability that the ball will not land in any slot two or more times. Let $\overline{A}$ be the event that the ball will not land in any slot two or more times. The events A and $\overline{A}$ are mutually exclusive and together they form the whole sample space. Then, by the Axioms 1 and 3, you have $P(A \text{ or } \overline{A}) = 1$ and $P(A \text{ or } \overline{A}) = P(A) + P(\overline{A})$. Thus

$$P(A) = 1 - P(\overline{A}).$$

This is the *complement rule*. The number of outcomes $(i_1, i_2, \ldots, i_7)$ for which all the i_k's are different is $37 \times 36 \times \cdots \times 31$. If you divide this number of outcomes by the total number of possible outcomes, then you find

$$P(\overline{A}) = \frac{37 \times 36 \times \cdots \times 31}{37^7} = 0.5466,$$

---

[3]The 1654 Pascal–Fermat correspondence marks the beginning of modern probability theory. In this correspondence another famous probability problem was solved. Chevalier de Méré had also brought to Pascal's attention the problem of points, in which the question is how the winnings of a game of chance should be divided between two players if the game was ended prematurely. This problem will be discussed in section 3.1.

or, rather $P(A) = 0.4534$. Would you have imagined that this probability would turn out to be so high?

Problem 2.1. A dog has a litter of four puppies. Use an appropriate sample space to verify that it is more likely that the litter consists of three puppies of the same gender and one of the other than that it consists of two puppies of each gender. (answer: the probabilities are $\frac{8}{16}$ and $\frac{6}{16}$)

Problem 2.2. Use an appropriate sample space in order to argue that the probability of getting at least one six in r rolls of a single die is $1 - \frac{5^r}{6^r}$, and the probability of getting at least one double six in r rolls of two dice is $1 - \frac{35^r}{36^r}$. What are the smallest values of r for which the two probabilities are more than 0.5? (answer: $r = 4$ and $r = 25$)

Problem 2.3. Eight heads of state, including the presidents of China and the U.S., are present at a summit conference. For the perfunctory group photo, the eight dignitaries are lined up randomly next to one other. Use an appropriate sample space to find the probability that the presidents of China and the U.S. will stand next to each other. (answer: $\frac{1}{4}$)

Problem 2.4. What is the probability of rolling two or more times a same number in a roll of three dice? (answer: $\frac{4}{9}$)

Problem 2.5. You are dealt 5 cards from a standard deck of 52 cards. What is the probability of getting at least one ace? (answer: 0.3412)

Problem 2.6. In a game show, a couple is presented with three closed doors, behind which, in random order, they will find a car, the key to the car, and a goat. One of the two players is given the task of finding the car, the other must find the car key. If both are successful, they get to keep the car. Each of the two players may open two doors; the second player may not see what is behind the doors chosen by the first player. The couple may discuss a strategy before the game starts. The strategy is that the player assigned with the task of finding the car opens door number 1 first. If that player finds the key (goat) behind door number 1, the player goes on to open door number 2 (3). The player assigned with the task of finding the key opens door number 2 first, and if player finds the car (goat) there, the player goes on to open door number 1 (3). Specify first a sample space and next calculate the probability of winning the car. (answer: $\frac{4}{6}$)

Problem 2.7. The sum rule is $P(A \text{ or } B) = P(A) + P(B) - P(A \text{ and } B)$ if the sets A and B are not disjoint. Can you explain this rule?

Problem 2.8. You throw a dart at a circular dartboard with radius R. The dart lands on a random point on the dartboard. What is the probability of the dart hitting the bull's-eye having radius b? (answer: b^2/R^2)

Problem 2.9. Two people have agreed to meet at the train station. Independently of one other, each person is to appear at a random moment between 12 p.m and 1 p.m. What is the probability that the two persons will meet within 10 minutes of each other? (answer: $\frac{11}{36}$)

2.2 The concept of conditional probability

The concept of conditional probability lies at the heart of probability theory. It is an intuitive concept. To illustrate this, most people reason as follows to find the probability of getting two aces when two cards are selected at random from an ordinary deck of 52 cards. The probability of getting an ace on the first card is $\frac{4}{52}$. Given that one ace is gone from the deck, the probability of getting an ace on the second card is $\frac{3}{51}$. Therefore

$$P(\text{the first two cards are aces}) = \frac{4}{52} \times \frac{3}{51}.$$

What is applied here is the *product rule* for probabilities:

$$P(A \text{ and } B) = P(A)P(B \mid A),$$

where $P(A$ and $B)$ stands for the probability that both event A ('the first card is an ace') and event B ('the second card is an ace') will occur, $P(B \mid A)$ is the notation for the conditional probability that event B will occur given that event A has occurred.[4] In words, the unconditional probability that both event A and event B will occur is equal to the unconditional probability that event A will occur times the conditional probability that event B will occur given that event A has occurred. This is one of the most useful rules in probability.

Example 2.5. Someone is looking to rent an apartment on the top floor of a certain building. The person gets wind of the fact that two apartments in the building have been vacated, and are up for rent. The building has seven floors, with eight apartments per floor. What is the probability of one of the vacant apartments being located on the top floor?

Solution. There are two possible approaches to solving this problem. In both, the complement rule is applied. This means that, instead of calculating the probability in question, you calculate the complementary probability of no top floor apartment being available. Once you know that, the sought-after probability is 1 minus that complementary probability.

Approach 1: This approach is based on counting and requires the specification of a sample space. The elements of the sample space are all possible combinations of two of the 56 apartments. The total number of possible combinations is $\binom{56}{2} = 1\,540$, whereas the number of possible combinations without a vacant apartment on the top floor

---

[4]In fact, the other way around, $P(B \mid A)$ is defined by $P(A$ and $B)/P(A)$. This definition can be motivated as follows. Suppose that n physically independent repetitions of a chance experiment are done under the same conditions. Let r be the number of times that event A occurs simultaneously with event B and s be the number of times that event A occurs but not event B. The frequency at which event B occurs in the cases that event A has occurred is equal to $\frac{r}{r+s}$. The frequency at which both event A and event B occur is $\frac{r}{n}$, and the frequency at which event A occurs is $\frac{r+s}{n}$. The ratio of these frequencies is $\frac{r}{r+s}$. This ratio is exactly the frequency at which event B occurs in the cases that event A has occurred, which explains the definition of the conditional probability $P(B \mid A)$.

is $\binom{48}{2} = 1\,128$. Then,

$$P(\text{no apartment is vacant on the top floor}) = \frac{1\,128}{1\,540} = 0.7325.$$

Approach 2: This approach is based on conditional probabilities and uses the trick of imagining that events occur sequentially in time. Imagine that the two available apartments were vacated one after the other. Then, let A be the event that the first vacant apartment is not located on the top floor and B be the event that the second vacant apartment is not located on the top floor. Using the formula $P(A \text{ and } B) = P(A)P(B \mid A)$, you find

$$P(\text{no apartment is vacant on the top floor}) = \frac{48}{56} \times \frac{47}{55} = 0.7325.$$

Example 2.6. Three boys and three girls are planning a dinner party. They agree that two of them will do the washing up, and they draw lots to determine which two it will be. What is the probability that two boys will wind up doing the washing up?

Solution. A useful solution strategy in probability is to see whether your problem is not the same as another problem, for which the solution is more obvious. This is the situation, here. The sought-after probability is the same as the probability of getting two red balls, when blindly choosing two balls from a bowl containing three red and three blue balls. If A represents the event that the first ball chosen is red, and B represents the event that the second ball chosen is red, then the sought-after probability is equal to $P(A \text{ and } B)$. Using the formula $P(A \text{ and } B) = P(A)P(B \mid A)$, you find

$$P(\text{two boys will do the washing up}) = \frac{3}{6} \times \frac{2}{5} = \frac{1}{5}.$$

Example 2.7. What is the probability that you have to pick five or more cards from a well-shuffled deck of 52 cards before you get an ace?

Solution. The solution uses a natural extension of the product rule. Noting that the sought-after probability is nothing else than the probability of getting no ace among the first four picked cards, let A_i be the event that the ith picked card is not an ace for $i = 1, \ldots, 4$. The probability $P(A_1 \text{ and } A_2 \text{ and } A_3 \text{ and } A_4)$ is calculated as

$$P(A_1) \times P(A_2 \mid A_1) \times P(A_3 \mid A_1 \text{ and } A_2) \times P(A_4 \mid A_1 \text{ and } A_2 \text{ and } A_3).$$

So the probability that five or more cards are needed to get an ace is

$$P(\text{no ace among the first four cards}) = \frac{48}{52} \times \frac{47}{51} \times \frac{46}{50} \times \frac{45}{49} = 0.7187.$$

The examples above show that when you use an approach based on conditional probabilities to solve the problem, you go straight to work without first defining a sample space. The counting approach, however, does require the specification of a sample space. If both approaches are possible for a given problem, then the approach based on conditional probabilities will, in general, be simpler than the counting approach.

To conclude this section, it is remarked that the formula

$$P(B \mid A) = \frac{P(A \text{ and } B)}{P(A)}$$

quantifies the fact that probabilities depend on the available information and change when additional information becomes available. As an illustration, suppose that two fair dice are rolled. What is the probability of a sum 8 given that the two dice have been landed on different numbers? Let A be the event that the two dice land on different numbers and B be the event that the sum is 8. Then $P(A) = \frac{30}{36}$ and $P(A \text{ and } B) = \frac{4}{36}$ (verify!). Then, $P(B \mid A) = \frac{4/36}{30/36} = \frac{2}{15}$, which differs from the original $P(B) = \frac{5}{36}$.

Problem 2.10. Five friends are sitting at a table in a restaurant. Two of them order white wine and the other three order red wine. The waiter has forgotten who ordered what and puts the drinks in random order before the five persons. What is the probability that each person gets the correct drink? (answer: $\frac{1}{10}$)

Problem 2.11. Two black socks, two brown socks and one white sock lie mixed up in a drawer. You grab two socks without looking.

What is the probability that you have grabbed two socks of the same color? (answer: $\frac{1}{5}$)

Problem 2.12. A bag contains 14 red cards and 7 black cards. You pick two cards at random from the bag. Verify that it is more likely to pick one red and one black card rather than two red cards. (answer: the probabilities are $\frac{14}{30}$ and $\frac{13}{30}$)

Problem 2.13. In the lotto 6/45 six different numbers are randomly drawn from the numbers 1 to 45. What is the probability that all six numbers drawn are larger than 10? (answer: 0.1993)

Problem 2.14. If you pick at random two children from the Johnson family, the chances are 50% that both children have blue eyes. How many children does the John family have and how many of them have blue eyes? (answer: 4 and 3)

Problem 2.15. Four British teams are among the eight teams that have reached the quarter-finals of the Champions League soccer. What is the probability that the four British teams will avoid each other in the quarter-finals draw if the eight teams are paired randomly? *Hint*: think of a bowl containing four red and four blue balls, where you remove each time two randomly chosen balls from the bowl. What is the probability that you remove each time a red and a blue ball? As noted before, finding the solution of a probability problem becomes often simpler by casting the problem in another form. (answer: $\frac{8}{35}$)

Problem 2.16. Someone has rolled two dice out of your sight. You ask this person to answer 'yes or no' on the question whether there is a six among the two rolls. He truthfully answers 'yes'. What is the probability that two sixes have been rolled? (answer: $\frac{1}{11}$)

Problem 2.17. Your friend shakes thoroughly two dice in a dice-box. He then looks into the dice-box. Your friend is honest and always tells you if he sees a six in which case he bets with even odds that both dice show an even number. Is the game favorable to you? (answer: yes, your probability of winning is $\frac{6}{11}$)

2.3 The law of conditional probability

Suppose that a closed box contains one ball. This ball is white. An extra ball is added to the box and the added ball is white or red with equal chances. Next one ball is blindly removed from the box. What is the probability that the removed ball is white? A natural reasoning is as follows. The probability of removing a white ball is 1 if a white ball has been added to the box and is $\frac{1}{2}$ if a red ball has been added to the box. It is intuitively reasonable to average these conditional probabilities over the probability that a white ball has been added and the probability that a red ball has been added. The latter two probabilities are both equal to $\frac{1}{2}$. Therefore

$$P(\text{the removed ball is white}) = 1 \times \frac{1}{2} + \frac{1}{2} \times \frac{1}{2} = \frac{3}{4}.$$

This is an application of the *law of conditional probability*. This law calculates a probability $P(A)$ with the help of appropriately chosen conditioning events B_1 and B_2. These events should be such that event A can occur only if one of the events B_1 and B_2 has occurred, and they should be mutually exclusive (that is, no more than one of the events B_1 and B_2 can occur at the same time). Then, $P(A)$ can be calculated as

$$P(A) = P(A \mid B_1)P(B_1) + P(A \mid B_2)P(B_2).$$

This is a very useful rule to calculate probabilities.[5] The extension of the rule to more than two conditioning events B_i is obvious. In general, the choice of the conditioning events is self-evident. In the above example, A is the event of drawing a white ball from the box when it contains two balls, B_1 is the event that a white ball has been added to the box and B_2 is the event that a red ball has been added. The power of conditioning is also illustrated by the next example.

Example 2.8. A drunkard removes two randomly chosen letters of the message HAPPY HOUR that is attached on a billboard outside

---

[5]The proof is simple. Since A can only occur if one of the events B_1 or B_2 has occurred and the events B_1 and B_2 are disjoint, $P(A) = P(A \text{ and } B_1) + P(A \text{ and } B_2)$ (by Axiom 3 in section 2.1). The product rule next leads to $P(A) = P(A \mid B_1)P(B_1) + P(A \mid B_2)P(B_2)$.

a pub. His drunk friend puts the two letters back in a random order. What is the probability that HAPPY HOUR appears again?

Solution. Let A be the event that HAPPY HOUR appears again. In order to calculate $P(A)$, it is obvious to condition on the two events B_1 and B_2, where B_1 is the event that two identical letters have been removed and B_2 is the event that two different letters have been removed. In order to apply the law of conditional probability, you need to know the probabilities $P(B_1)$, $P(B_2)$, $P(A \mid B_1)$ and $P(A \mid B_2)$. The latter two probabilities are easy: $P(A \mid B_1) = 1$ and $P(A \mid B_2) = \frac{1}{2}$. The probabilities $P(B_1)$ and $P(B_2)$ require some more thought. It suffices to determine $P(B_1)$, because $P(B_2) = 1 - P(B_1)$. The probability $P(B_1)$ is the sum of the probability that the drunkard has removed the two H's and the probability that the drunkard has removed the P's. Each of the latter two probabilities is equal to $\frac{2}{9} \times \frac{1}{8} = \frac{1}{36}$, by the product rule. Thus $P(B_1) = \frac{1}{18}$ and $P(B_2) = \frac{17}{18}$. By the law of conditional probability, $P(A) = 1 \times \frac{1}{18} + \frac{1}{2} \times \frac{17}{18} = \frac{19}{36}$. Thus

$$P(\text{the message HAPPPY HOUR appears again}) = \frac{19}{36}.$$

Problem 2.18. Michael arrives home on time with probability 0.8. If Michael does not arrive home on time, the probability that his dinner is burnt is 0.5; otherwise, his dinner is burnt with probability 0.15. What is the probability that Michael's dinner will be burnt? (answer: 0.22)

Problem 2.19. Your friend has chosen at random a card from a standard deck of 52 cards, but keeps this card concealed. You have to guess what card it is. Before doing so, you can ask your friend either the question whether the chosen card is red or the question whether the card is the ace of spades. Your friend will answer truthfully. What question would you ask? (answer: the probability of a correct guess is $\frac{1}{26}$ in both cases)

Problem 2.20. One fish is contained in an opaque fishbowl. The fish is equally likely to be a piranha or a goldfish. A sushi lover throws a piranha into the fish bowl alongside the other fish. Then, immediately, before either fish can devour the other, one of the fish is blindly removed from the fishbowl. The removed fish appears to be a piranha. What is the probability that the fish that was originally in the bowl by itself was a piranha? (answer: $\frac{2}{3}$)

Problem 2.21. In a lotto 6/45 drawing, six different numbers are randomly drawn from the numbers 1 to 45. You win the jackpot if you have predicted correctly all six numbers drawn. If you have exactly two numbers correctly predicted on a ticket, you get a free ticket for the next lotto drawing. What is the probability that you will ever win the jackpot when you buy for once and for all a single ticket for playing in the lotto? (answer: 1.447×10^{-7})

Problem 2.22. On the TV show 'Deal or No Deal', you are faced with 26 briefcases in which various amounts of money have been placed including the amounts \$2 500 000 and \$1 000 000. You first choose one case. This case is 'yours' and is kept out of play until the very end of the game. Then you play the game and in each round you open several cases. What is the probability that the cases with \$2 500 000 and \$1 000 000 will be still unopened at the end of the game when you are going to open 20 cases? (answer: $\frac{3}{65}$)

2.4 Conditional probability and Bayesian probability

The Bayesian view of probability is interwoven with conditional probability. Bayes' formula, which is nothing else than logical thinking, is the most important rule in Bayesian probability.[6] To introduce this rule, consider again Problem 2.18. In this problem, Michael finds his dinner burnt (event A) with probability 0.5 if he does not arrive home on time (event B). That is, $P(A \mid B) = 0.5$. Suppose you are asked to give the probability $P(B \mid A)$, being the conditional probability that Michael did not arrive home on time given that his

---

[6]This formula is named after the English clergyman Thomas Bayes (1702–1762) who derived a special case of the formula. The formula in its general form was first written down by the famous French scientist Pierre Simon Laplace (1749–1827). Bayes' formula laid the foundation for a separate branch of statistics, namely Bayesian statistics.

dinner is burnt. In fact you are asked to reason back from effect to cause. Then, you are in the area of Bayesian probability. The *basic form of Bayes' rule* is

$$P(B \mid A) = \frac{P(B)P(A \mid B)}{P(A)}$$

for any two events A and B with $P(A) > 0$. The derivation of this formula is strikingly simple. The basic form of Bayes' rule follows directly from the definition of conditional probability:

$$P(B \mid A) = \frac{P(B \text{ and } A)}{P(A)} = \frac{P(B)P(A \mid B)}{P(A)}.$$

In Problem 2.18, the probabilities $P(B)$ and $P(A \mid B)$ had known values 0.2 and 0.5, and, using the law of conditional probability, the probability $P(A)$ was calculated as 0.22. Thus the probability that Michael did not arrive home on time given that his dinner is burnt is equal to

$$P(B \mid A) = \frac{0.2 \times 0.5}{0.22} = \frac{5}{11}.$$

You see that Bayes' rule enables you to reason back from effect to cause in terms of probabilities.

There are various versions for Bayes' rule. The most insightful version is the Bayes' rule in odds form. This version is mostly used in practice. Before stating Bayes' rule in odds form, the concept of '*odds*' will be discussed. Let G be any event that will occur with probability p, and so event G will not occur with probability $1 - p$. Then the odds of event G are defined by:

$$o(G) = \frac{p}{1 - p}.$$

Conversely, the odds $o(G)$ of an event G determine the probability p of event G occurring:

$$p = \frac{o(G)}{1 + o(G)}.$$

For example, an event G with probability $\frac{2}{3}$ has odds 2 (it is often said the odds are 2:1 in favor of event G), while an event with odds $\frac{2}{9}$ (odds are 2:9) has a probability $\frac{2}{11}$ of occurring.

For reasons that will become clear in a few moments, Bayes' rule in odds form will work with events E and H rather than A and B. Also, the standard notation $\overline{H}$ is used for the event that event H does not occur. Then, the *Bayes' rule in odds form* reads as[7]

$$\frac{P(H \mid E)}{P(\overline{H} \mid E)} = \frac{P(H)}{P(\overline{H})} \times \frac{P(E \mid H)}{P(E \mid \overline{H})}.$$

This formula is one of the most useful formulas in probability theory. What does this formula say and how to use it? This is easiest explained with the help of an example.

Suppose that a team of divers believes that a sought-after wreck will be in a certain sea area with a probability of $p = 0.4$. A search in that area will detect the wreck with a probability of $d = 0.9$ if it is there. What is the revised probability of the wreck being in the area when the area is searched and no wreck is found? To answer this question, let hypothesis H be the event that the wreck is in the area in question and thus $\overline{H}$ is the event that the wreck is not in that area. Before the search takes place, the events H and $\overline{H}$ have probabilities $P(H) = 0.4$ and $P(\overline{H}) = 0.6$. These probabilities are called *prior probabilities*. The ratio of $P(H)$ and $P(\overline{H})$ is the *prior odds* of hypothesis H. These odds will change if additional information becomes available. Denote by evidence E the event that the search is not successful. The probability $P(E \mid H) = 1 - 0.9 = 0.1$. Obviously, the probability $P(E \mid \overline{H}) = 1$. The ratio of $P(E \mid H)$ and $P(E \mid \overline{H})$ is called the *likelihood ratio* or *Bayes factor*. It will be clear that the evidence supports the hypothesis if the likelihood ratio is greater than 1 and supports the negation of the hypothesis if the likelihood ratio is less than 1. Once the prior odds and the likelihood factor have been determined, Bayes' rule in odds form can be applied to calculate the *posterior odds* of hypothesis H. These posterior odds are $o(H \mid E) = P(H \mid E)/P(\overline{H} \mid E)$. The *posterior probability* of hypothesis H follows directly from these posterior odds

---

[7]This rule is obtained as follows. The basic form of the formula of Bayes gives that $P(H \mid E) = P(H)P(E \mid H)/P(E)$ and $P(\overline{H} \mid E) = P(\overline{H})P(E \mid \overline{H})/P(E)$. Taking the ratio of these two expressions, $P(E)$ cancels out and you get Bayes' rule in odds form.

and is given by:

$$P(H \mid E) = \frac{o(H \mid E)}{1 + o(H \mid E)}.$$

The posterior probability $P(H \mid E)$ gives the updated value of the probability that hypothesis H is true after that additional information has become available through the evidence event E. Going back to the search for the wreck, Bayes' rule in odds form gives that the posterior odds of the event that the wreck is in the area in question is equal to:

$$\frac{P(H \mid E)}{P(\overline{H} \mid E)} = \frac{0.4}{0.6} \times \frac{0.1}{1} = \frac{1}{15}.$$

Thus the posterior probability of hypothesis H is

$$P(H \mid E) = \frac{1/15}{1 + 1/15} = \frac{1}{16}.$$

This is the revised value of the probability that the wreck is in the area in question after the futile search.

In words, Bayes' rule in odds form is often stated as:

posterior odds = prior odds × likelihood ratio.

It is emphasized that the prior odds of hypothesis H refer to the situation *before* the occurrence of evidence event E and that the posterior odds of hypothesis H refer to the situation *after* the occurrence of event E.

Example 2.9. An athlete selected by lot has to go to the doping control. On average, 7 out of 100 athletes use doping. The doping test gives a positive result with a probability of 96% if the athlete has used doping and with a probability of 5% if the athlete has not used doping. Suppose that the athlete gets a negative test result. What is the probability that the athlete has nevertheless used doping?

Solution. Let the hypothesis H be the event that the athlete has used doping. The prior probabilities are $P(H) = 0.07$ and $P(\overline{H}) = 0.93$. Let E be the event that the athlete has a negative test result.

Then, $P(E \mid H) = 0.04$ and $P(E \mid \overline{H}) = 0.95$. The posterior odds of the hypothesis H are

$$\frac{P(H \mid E)}{P(\overline{H} \mid E)} = \frac{0.07}{0.93} \times \frac{0.04}{0.95} = 0.003169.$$

Thus the revised value of the probability of doping use notwithstanding a negative test result is

$$P(H \mid E) = \frac{0.003169}{1 + 0.003169} = 0.003159,$$

or, rather about 0.32%. A very small probability indeed.

The posterior probability of 0.32% can also be calculated without using conditional probabilities and Bayes' rule. The alternative calculation is based on the method of expected frequencies. This method is also easy to understand by the layman. Imagine a very large number of athletes that are selected by lot for the doping control, say 10 000 athletes. On average 700 of these athletes have used doping and on average 9 300 athletes have not used doping. Of these 700 athletes, $700 \times 0.04 = 28$ athletes test negative on average, whereas $9\,300 \times 0.95 = 8\,835$ athletes of the other 9 300 athletes test negative on average. Thus a total of $28 + 8\,835 = 8\,863$ athletes test negative and among those 8 863 athletes there are 28 doping users. Therefore the probability that an athlete has used doping notwithstanding a negative test result is

$$\frac{28}{8\,863} = 0.003159.$$

The same probability as found with Bayes' rule. A similar reasoning shows that the probability that an athlete with a positive test result has not used doping is $\frac{465}{465+672} = 0.40987$ (verify!).

In the following problems you are asked to apply Bayes' rule in odds form. You should first identify the hypothesis H and the evidence E.

Problem 2.23. An oil explorer performs a seismic test to determine whether oil is likely to be found in a certain area. The probability that the test indicates the presence of oil is 90% if oil is indeed present in the test area, while the probability of a false positive is 15% if no oil is present in the test area. Before the test is done, the explorer believes that the probability of presence of oil in the test area is 40%. What is the revised probability of oil being present in the test area given that the test is positive? (answer: 0.8)

Problem 2.24. Consider Problem 2.18 again. What is the probability that Michael arrived at home on time given that he did not find his dinner burnt? (answer: $\frac{34}{39}$)

Problem 2.25. On the island of liars each inhabitant lies with probability $\frac{2}{3}$. You overhear an inhabitant making a statement. Next you ask another inhabitant whether the inhabitant you overheard spoke truthfully. What is the probability that the inhabitant you overheard indeed spoke truthfully given that the other inhabitant says so? (answer: $\frac{1}{5}$)

Problem 2.26. A doctor discovers a lump in a woman's breast during a routine physical exam. The lump could be a cancer. Without performing any further tests, the probability that the woman has breast cancer is 0.01. A further test can be done. On average, this test is correctly able to establish whether a tumor is benign or cancerous 90% of the time. A positive test result indicates that a tumor is cancerous. What is the probability that the woman has breast cancer if the test result is positive? (answer: $\frac{1}{12}$)

Problem 2.27. You have two symmetric dice in your pocket. One die is a standard die and the other die has each of the three numbers 2, 4, and 6 twice on its faces. You random pick one die from your pocket without looking. Someone else rolls this die and informs you that a 6 has shown up. What is the revised value of the probability that you have picked the standard die? How does this probability change if the die is rolled a second time and a 6 appears again? (answer: $\frac{1}{3}$ and $\frac{1}{5}$)

Problem 2.28. There are two taxicab companies in a particular city, 'Yellow Cabs' and 'White Cabs'. Of all cabs in the city, 85%

are 'Yellow Cabs' and 15% are 'White Cabs'. On a rainy evening
there was a hit-and-run accident with a taxicab. A witness believes
that it was a 'White Cab'. In order to test witness reliability, the
court of law has set up a test situation similar to the one occurring
on the night of the hit-and-run accident. Results showed that 80%
of the participants in the test case correctly identified the cab color,
while 20% of the participants identified the wrong company. What is
the probability that the accused hit-and-run cabbie is a White Cabs
employee? (answer: $\frac{12}{29}$)

The case Sally Clark: a miscarriage of justice

Sally Clark was arrested in 1999 after her second child of a few months
old died, ostensibly by cot death, just as her first child had died a year
earlier. She was accused of suffocating both children. During the trial
the prosecutor called a famous pediatrician as an expert. He stated that
the chance of cot death of a child was about 1 in 8 543 and stated that
the chance of two cot deaths in the same family was $\left(\frac{1}{8\,543}\right)^2$, or, about
1 in 73 million. The prosecutor argued that, beyond any reasonable
doubt, Sally Clark was guilty of murdering her two children, and the jury
sentenced her to life imprisonment, though there was no other evidence
that Sally Clark had killed her two children. This is a classic example of
the 'prosecutor's fallacy'. The probability of innocence given the death
of the two children – the probability that matters – is confused with the
tiny probability that in the same family two children of a few months
old will die of sudden infant death syndrome.

    The conviction of Sally Clark led to great controversy and several
leading British statisticians threw themselves into the case. The statisticians came up with various estimates for Sally Clark's chance of innocence and all these estimates showed that the condemnation of her
was not beyond reasonable doubt. The formula of Bayes was the basis
of the calculations of the statisticians. How did this work? Let H be
the event that Sally Clark is guilty and the evidence E be the event
that both of her children died in the first few months of their lives. The
probability that matters is the conditional probability $P(H \mid E)$. To get
this probability, you need prior probabilities $P(H)$ and $P(\overline{H})$ together
with likelihood ratio $P(E \mid H)/P(E \mid \overline{H})$. The assumption is made
that murder by the mother (hypothesis H) and cot death (hypothesis

$\overline{H}$) are the only two possibilities for the death of the two children. Of course, $P(E \mid H) = 1$. The pediatrician, called as an expert, gave the estimate $\frac{1}{8543} \times \frac{1}{8543}$ for $P(E \mid \overline{H})$, but this estimate assumes independence between both deaths. However, a cot death in a family increases the likelihood that a subsequent birth in the family will also die of cot death. In an article in the British Medical Journal it was made plausible that a factor of 5 applies to the increased chance. Thus the probability $P(E \mid \overline{H})$ is estimated by

$$P(E \mid \overline{H}) = \frac{1}{8\,543} \times \frac{5}{8\,543} \approx 6.85 \times 10^{-8},$$

or, about 1 in 14.8 million, which is still a very small probability. However, this probability should be weighed with the very small prior probability that a mother will kill her both children at the beginning of their first year of life by suffocation. How do you get a good estimate for the prior probability $P(H)$? This is not simple. However, on the basis of statistical data, an upper bound for the prior probability $P(H)$ can be estimated. Instead of asking how often mothers in a family like the Clarks kill their first two children in their first year of life, the question can be answered how often mothers kill one or more of their children of any age. Data are available in the U.S. Statistics give about 100 cases per year in the U.S. In the U.S. there are about 120 million adult women and about half of them have children, so about 1 in 0.6 million American women murder one or more of their children. The frequency of murders in America is about 4 times as large as in England. This leads to the estimate that about 1 in 2.4 million women in England kill one or more of their children. This is, of course, an overestimate of the prior probability $P(H)$. If you nevertheless take

$$P(H) = \frac{1}{2.4 \times 10^6},$$

then you find with Bayes' rule in odds form that

$$\frac{P(H \mid E)}{P(\overline{H} \mid E)} \approx \frac{1/(2.4 \times 10^{-6})}{1 - 1/(2.4 \times 10^{-6})} \times \frac{1}{6.85 \times 10^{-8}} \approx 6.08.$$

This gives
$$P(H \mid E) \approx 6.08/(1 + 6.08) = 0.859.$$

The probability 0.859 is an overestimate for the probability that Sally Clark is guilty. The explanation that the probability 0.859 overestimates the probability of guilt is based on the fact that, for any numbers p and q between 0 and 1,

$$\frac{p}{1-p} < \frac{q}{1-q} \text{ if } p < q \text{ and, conversely, } p < q \text{ if } \frac{p}{1-p} < \frac{q}{1-q}$$

(verify!). So a probability of 14.1% or more is a reasonable estimate for the probability of Sally Clark's innocence. This is of course no base for a conviction when there is no other evidence. Despite the arguments that statisticians presented, Sally Clark lost the appeal against her conviction. But in 2003 she was acquitted after it came out that her second child had a bacterial infection in the brain at the time of his death, a fact that was abstained from the defense in the earlier trial. The tragic event surrounding Sally Clark is similar with the miscarriage of justice that took place in the Netherlands around the nurse Lucia de Berk who was wrongly accused of murdering a number of her patients who died during her night shifts.

Bayesian statistics

Bayesian probability is the basis of Bayesian statistics. This field of statistics is very different from the field of classical statistics dealing with hypothesis-testing. Imagine that a new medication is being tested on a given number of patients, and that it appears to be effective for a number of them. You want to know if this means that the medication works. In classical statistics, you would start with the assumption that mere fluke is the cause of the test results (this is called the null hypothesis). The null hypothesis is then tested using the so-called p-value, being the probability of getting data that are *at least* as good as the observed data if the null hypothesis would be true. If the p-value is below some threshold value – the value 0.05 is often used as a cut-off value – the null hypothesis is rejected and it is assumed that the medication is effective (it is said that the findings are 'statistically significant'). The p-value, however, does not tell you what the probability is that the new medication is not effective. And this is, in fact, the probability you really want to know. Scientific studies have shown that the p-value can give a highly distorted picture of this probability. The probability that the medication is not effective can be considerably larger than the p-value. As a consequence, you must careful with drawing a conclusion when the p-value is just below 0.05; the test $p < 0.05$ is not a litmus test. As such the test was never intended, but it was meant as a signal to investigate matters further.

Bayesian statistics enables you to give a judgment about the probability that the medication works. The judgment is based on the generic formula:

$$p(\theta \mid data) = \frac{p(data \mid \theta)p(\theta)}{p(data)}.$$

What is the meaning of the elements of this formula? This formula determines the posterior probability distribution $p(\theta \mid data)$ of an unknown parameter θ. For example, you can think of θ as the percentage of people for whom a new medication is working. To estimate the posterior distribution, you need data from test experiments. Before the tests are done, you should specify a prior probability distribution $p(\theta)$ on the parameter θ. The (subjective) prior probabilities represent the uncertainty in your knowledge about the true value of θ. The use of priors distinguishes Bayesian statistics from classical statistics. The so-called likelihood $p(data \mid \theta)$ is the probability of finding the observed data for a given value of θ, and $p(data)$ is obtained by averaging $p(data \mid \theta)$ over the prior probabilities $p(\theta)$. This describes in general terms how Bayesian statistics works. The Bayesian approach is used more and more in practice. Nowadays, Bayesian methods are used widely to address pressing questions in diverse application areas such as astrophysics, actuarial sciences, neurobiology, weather forecasting, spam filtering and criminal justice.

2.5 The concept of random variable

In performing a chance experiment, one is often not interested in the particular outcome that occurs but in a specific numerical value associated with that outcome. Any function that assigns a real number to each outcome in the sample space of the experiment is called a *random variable*.

The concept of random variable is always a difficult concept for the beginner. A random variable is not a variable in the traditional sense of the word and actually it is a little misleading to call it a variable. Intuitively, a random variable is a function that takes on its value by chance. Formally, a random variable is defined as a function that assigns a numerical value to each element of the sample space. The observed value, or realization, of a random variable is completely determined by the realized outcome of the chance experiment and consequently probabilities can be assigned to the possible values of the random variable. A random variable gets its value only *after* the chance experiment has been done. *Before* the chance experiment is done, you can only speak of the probability that the random variable will take on a particular value. It is common to use uppercase letters such as X, Y, and Z to denote random variables, and lowercase letters x, y, and z to denote their possible numerical values.

You have *discrete* and *continuous* random variables. A discrete random variable can take on only a finite or a countably infinite number of values, whereas a continuous random variable has a continuum of possible values (think of an interval). The number of goals to be scored in a soccer game is a discrete random variable, but the time until radioactive material will emit a particle is a continuous random variable. In this book the emphasis is on discrete random variables, but section 3.2 will deal with the continuous normal and exponential distributions.

Suppose that $a_1, a_2, \ldots, a_r$ are the possible values of a discrete random variable X. The notation $P(X = a_k)$ is used for the probability that the random variable X will take on the value a_k. The probabilities $P(X = a_k)$ for $k = 1, \ldots, r$ form the so-called *probability mass function* of the random variable X and should satisfy $\sum_{k=1}^{r} P(X = a_k) = 1$.

Example 2.10. Let the random variable X be the sum of points to be obtained in a single roll of two fair dice. What is the probability mass function of X?

Solution. As in Example 2.1, it is helpful to think of a blue die and a red die. The sample space of the chance experiment consists of the 36 outcomes (i, j) for $i, j = 1, \ldots, 6$, where i is the number rolled by the blue die and j is the number rolled by the red die. Each outcome is equally likely and gets assigned a probability of $\frac{1}{36}$. The random variable X takes on the value $i + j$ when the realized outcome is (i, j). The possible values of X are 2 to 12. To find the probability $P(X = k)$, you must know the outcomes (i, j) for which the random variable X takes on the value k. For example, X takes on the value 7 for the outcomes $(1, 6)$, $(2, 5)$, $(3, 4)$, $(4, 3)$, $(5, 2)$, and $(6, 1)$. Each of these six outcomes has probability $\frac{1}{36}$. Thus $P(X = 7) = \frac{6}{36}$. Using this reasoning, you are asked to verify

$$P(X = j) = \begin{cases} (j - 1)/36 & \text{for } 2 \le j \le 7, \\ (13 - j)/36 & \text{for } 8 \le j \le 12. \end{cases}$$

Problem 2.29. Let the random variable X be the largest number rolled in a roll of two fair dice. What is the probability mass function of X? (answer: $P(X = j) = (2j - 1)/36$ for $j = 1, \dots, 6$)

Problem 2.30. In your pocket you have three dimes (coins of 10 cents) and two quarters (coins of 25 cents). Let the random variable X be the amount of cents in your hand if you grab at random two coins from your pocket. What is the probability mass function of X? (answer: 0.3, 0.6 and 0.1)

2.6 Expected value and standard deviation

Suppose that $a_1, a_2, \dots, a_r$ are the possible values of the discrete random variable X. The *expected value* (or *average value*) of the random variable X is defined by

$$E(X) = a_1 \times P(X = a_1) + a_2 \times P(X = a_2) + \dots + a_r \times P(X = a_r).$$

In words, $E(X)$ is a weighted average of the possible values that X can take on, where each value is weighted with the probability that X will take on that particular value.[8] The term 'expected value' can be misleading. This term should not be confused with the term 'most probable value'. An insurance salesman who tells a 35-year-old person that he or she can expect to live for another 43 years

---

[8]The idea of an expected value appears in the 1654 Pascal–Fermat correspondence and this idea was elaborated on by the Dutch astronomer Christiaan Huygens (1625–1695) in his famous 1657 book *Ratiociniis de Ludo Aleae* (On Reasoning in Games of Chance).

has certainly arrived at the number 43 by multiplying the possible values of the number of years the person has left to live with their corresponding probabilities, and then adding the products together. The expected value $E(X)$ is not necessarily a number that can be taken on by the random variable X. For example, think of X as the number of points achieved in one roll of a fair die. Then

$$E(X) = 1 \times \frac{1}{6} + 2 \times \frac{1}{6} + 3 \times \frac{1}{6} + 4 \times \frac{1}{6} + 5 \times \frac{1}{6} + 6 \times \frac{1}{6} = 3.5.$$

Why is the term average value also used for expected value? Suppose that you are repeatedly rolling a fair die. It will come as no surprise that the fraction of the number of rolls with outcome j goes to $\frac{1}{6}$ for all $j = 1, 2, \ldots, 6$ if the number of rolls gets larger and larger. This means that the average number points obtained per roll tends to $\frac{1}{6}(1 + 2 + \cdots + 6) = 3.5$ if the number of rolls gets very large, and the number 3.5 is precisely the expected value of the outcome of a single roll with the die.

In many practical problems, it is helpful to interpret the expected value of a random variable as a long-term average. This is the case in the following example, which describes an interesting application of the concept of expected value. The application has its origin in World War II when a large number of soldiers had their blood tested for syphilis.

Example 2.11. A large number of individuals must undergo a blood test for a certain disease. The probability that a randomly selected person will have the disease is $p = 0.005$. In order to reduce costs, it is decided that the large group should be split into smaller groups, each made up of r persons, after which the blood samples of the r persons will be pooled and tested as one. The pooled blood samples will only test negative (disease free) if all of the individual blood samples were negative. If a test returns a positive result, then all of the r samples from that group will be retested, individually. What is the expected value of the number of tests that will have to be performed on one group of r individuals?

Solution. Define the random variable X as the number of tests that will have to be performed on a group of r individuals. The random variable X has the two possible values 1 and $r + 1$. The probability that X will take on the value 1 is equal to the probability that each individual blood sample will test negative, and this probability is $(1 - p) \times (1 - p) \times \cdots \times (1 - p) = (1 - p)^r$. This means that $P(X = 1) = 0.995^r$ and $P(X = r + 1) = 1 - 0.995^r$. Therefore

$$E(X) = 1 \times 0.995^r + (r + 1) \times (1 - 0.995^r).$$

In other words, by pooling the blood samples of the r individuals, an average of $\frac{1}{r}\left(1 \times 0.995^r + (r + 1) \times (1 - 0.995^r)\right)$ tests per individual are needed.[9] This average can be calculated for various values of r and the average appears to be minimal for $r = 15$ with 0.1391 as minimum value. Thus the pooling of 15 individual blood samples saves about 86% on the number of tests necessary.

Example 2.12. You play the following game. A fair coin is tossed. If it lands heads, it will be tossed one more time; otherwise, it will be tossed two more times. You win eight dollars if heads does not come up at all, but you must pay one dollar each time heads does turn up. Is this a fair game?

Solution. The set $\{HH, HT, THH, THT, TTH, TTT\}$ is an obvious choice for the sample space, where H stands for heads and T for tails. The random variable X being defined as your net winnings in a game takes on the value 8 for outcome TTT, the value -1 for each of the outcomes HT, THT and TTH, and the value -2 for each of the outcomes HH and THH. The probability $\frac{1}{2} \times \frac{1}{2} = \frac{1}{4}$ is assigned to each of the outcomes HH and HT and the probability $\frac{1}{2} \times \frac{1}{2} \times \frac{1}{2} = \frac{1}{8}$ to each of the other four outcomes. Thus

$$P(X = 8) = \frac{1}{8}, \; P(X = -1) = \frac{1}{4} + \frac{1}{8} + \frac{1}{8}, \; \text{and } P(X = -2) = \frac{1}{4} + \frac{1}{8}.$$

This gives

$$E(X) = 8 \times \frac{1}{8} - 1 \times \frac{1}{2} - 2 \times \frac{3}{8} = -\frac{1}{4}.$$

---

[9]This fact is a special case of the strong law of large numbers, which is a fundamental result that can be proved from the simple axioms of probability theory. By this law, the average number of tests per group of r individuals will tend to the expected value $E(X)$ with probability one if the number of groups becomes indefinitely large.

The game is not fair. In the long run you will lose a quarter dollar per game.

Linearity property and the substitution formula

A very useful property of the expected value is the *linearity property*. This property states that

$$E(aX + bY) = aE(X) + bE(Y)$$

for any two random variables X and Y and any constants a and b, regardless whether or not there is dependence between X and Y. This result is valid for any type of random variables, as long as the expected values $E(X)$ en $E(Y)$ are well-defined. For the special case of discrete random variables each having only a finite number of possible values, a proof will be given in the appendix of this chapter.

Another important formula is the *substitution formula*, which will also be proved in the appendix. Suppose that $g(x)$ is a given function, say $g(x) = x^2$ or $g(x) = \sin(x)$. Then $g(X)$ is also a random variable when X is a random variable. If X is a discrete random variable with possible values $a_1, \ldots, a_r$, then the substitution formula tells you that the expected value of $g(X)$ can be calculated through the intuitively obvious formula

$$E[g(X)] = \sum_{j=1}^{r} g(a_j)P(X = a_j).$$

Thus you need not to know the probability mass function of the random variable $g(X)$ in order to calculate its expected value. This is a very useful result in probability. A special case of the substitution formula is

$$E(aX + b) = aE(X) + b \text{ for any constants } a \text{ and } b.$$

Variance and standard deviation

A measure for the variability of a random variable X around its expected value $\mu = E(X)$ is the *variance*. The variance of X is defined by

$$\text{var}(X) = E\big((X - \mu)^2\big).$$

The notation $\sigma^2(X)$ is often used for var(X). Alternatively, var(X) can be calculated as

$$\text{var}(X) = E(X^2) - \mu^2,$$

as can be seen by writing $(X - \mu)^2$ as $X^2 - 2\mu X + \mu^2$ and using the linearity property of expectation. In Problem 2.33 you are asked to verify that

$$\text{var}(aX + b) = a^2\text{var}(X) \text{ for any constants } a \text{ and } b.$$

Using the substitution formula, the variance of a discrete random variable X with $a_1, a_2, \ldots, a_r$ as possible values can be calculated as

$$\text{var}(X) = \sum_{j=1}^{r}(a_j-\mu)^2 P(X = a_j) \text{ or } \text{var}(X) = \sum_{j=1}^{r} a_j^2 P(X = a_j)-\mu^2.$$

The variance of a random variable X has not the same units (e.g., dollar or cm) as $E(X)$. For example, if X is expressed in dollars, then var(X) has (dollars)^2 as dimension. Therefore one often uses the *standard deviation* that is defined as the square root of the variance. The standard deviation of X is denoted by $\sigma(X)$ and is thus given by

$$\sigma(X) = \sqrt{\text{var}(X)}.$$

As an illustration, suppose that X is the number of points to be obtained in a single roll of a die. As seen above, $E(X) = 3.5$. The variance and standard deviation of X are given by

$$\text{var}(X) = \sum_{j=1}^{6}(j - 3.5)^2 \frac{1}{6} = \frac{35}{12} \text{ and } \sigma(X) = \sqrt{\frac{35}{12}}.$$

Example 2.13. Joe and his friend bet every week whether the Dow Jones index will have risen at the end of the week or not. Both put $10 in the pot. Joe observes that his friend is just guessing and is making his choice by the toss of a fair coin. Joe asks his friend if he could contribute $20 to the pot and submit his guess together with that of his brother. The friend agrees. In each week, however, Joe's brother submits a prediction opposite to that of Joe. If there is only one correct prediction, the entire pot goes to that prediction. If there is more than one correct prediction, the pot is split evenly between the correct predictions. How favorable is the game to Joe and his brother?

Solution. Let the random variable X denote the payoff to Joe and his brother in any given week. Either Joe or his brother will have a correct prediction. They win the \$30 pot if Joe's friend is wrong; otherwise, they share the pot with Joe's friend. Therefore the possible values of X are 30 and 15 dollars. Each of these two values is equally likely, since Joe's friend makes his prediction by the toss of a coin. This gives

$$E(X) = 30 \times \frac{1}{2} + 15 \times \frac{1}{2} = 22.5 \text{ dollars.}$$

In any week, Joe and his brother have an expected profit of $E(X - 20) = 2.5$ dollars. To obtain $\sigma(X)$, you first calculate

$$E(X^2) = 900 \times \frac{1}{2} + 225 \times \frac{1}{2} = 562.5 \text{ (dollars)}^2.$$

This gives $\text{var}(X) = 562.5 - 22.5^2 = 56.25$ (dollars)^2. Thus

$$\sigma(X) = \sqrt{56.25} = 7.5 \text{ dollars.}$$

Since $\sigma(X - 20) = \sigma(X)$, the standard deviation of the profit $X - 20$ for Joe and his brother is also equal to 7.5 dollars.

Variance of a sum of independent random variables

As seen above, $E(X + Y) = E(X) + E(Y)$ for any two random variables X and Y. A similar result for the variance is in general not true. You can see this from the example with $P(X = 1) = P(X = -1) = \frac{1}{2}$ and $Y = -X$. In this example, $\text{var}(X + Y) = 0$ and $\text{var}(X) = \text{var}(Y) = 1$ (verify!). The dependence between X and Y is the reason that $\text{var}(X + Y)$ is not equal to $\text{var}(X) + \text{var}(Y)$.

Independence of X and Y is required for equality.[10] If the random variables X and Y are independent of each other, then

$$\text{var}(aX + bY) = a^2\text{var}(X) + b^2\text{var}(Y)$$

for any constants a and b. This result is true for any type of random variables. For the special case of discrete random variables X and Y, a proof is given in the appendix to this chapter. More generally, if the random variables $X_1, \ldots, X_n$ are independent of each other, then

$$\text{var}(a_1X_1 + \cdots + a_nX_n) = a_1^2\,\text{var}(X_1) + \cdots + a_n^2\,\text{var}(X_n)$$

for all constants $a_1, \ldots, a_n$ and any $n \geq 2$.

As an illustration, what is the standard deviation of the sum of a roll of two dice? Let X be the number rolled on the first die and Y be the number rolled on the second die. The sum of a roll of two dice can is given by $X + Y$. As calculated before, $\text{var}(X) = \text{var}(Y) = \frac{35}{12}$. The random variables X and Y are independent of each other. Then $\text{var}(X + Y) = \text{var}(X) + \text{var}(Y) = \frac{35}{6}$. Thus the standard deviation of the sum of a roll of two dice is

$$\sigma(X + Y) = \sqrt{\frac{35}{6}} \approx 2.415 \text{ points.}$$

The expected value of the sum is $E(X + Y) = 3.5 + 3.5 = 7$.

The square root law for the standard deviation

Let $X_1, \ldots, X_n$ be independent random variables each having standard deviation σ. Then, by $\text{var}\left(\sum_{k=1}^n X_k\right) = \sum_{k=1}^n \text{var}(X_k) = n\sigma^2$ and $\text{var}\left(\frac{1}{n}\sum_{k=1}^n X_k\right) = \frac{1}{n^2}\sum_{k=1}^n \text{var}(X_k) = \frac{\sigma^2}{n}$, you find

$$\sigma\left(\sum_{k=1}^n X_k\right) = \sigma\sqrt{n} \quad \text{and} \quad \sigma\left(\frac{1}{n}\sum_{k=1}^n X_k\right) = \frac{\sigma}{\sqrt{n}}.$$

---

[10]If $P(X \leq x \text{ and } Y \leq y) = P(X \leq x)P(Y \leq y)$ for all x and y, then the random variables X and Y are said to be independent of each other. An alternative definition of independence is $P(X = x \text{ and } Y = y) = P(X = x)P(Y = y)$ for all x and y when X and Y are discrete random variables. In general, $X_1, \ldots, X_n$ are said to be independent of each other if $P(X_1 \leq x_1, \ldots, X_n \leq x_n) = P(X_1 \leq x_1) \cdots P(X_n \leq x_n)$ for all $x_1, x_2, \ldots, x_n$.

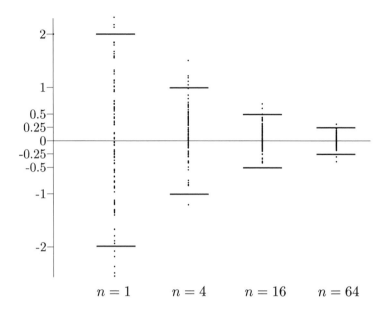

$$n = 1 \qquad n = 4 \qquad n = 16 \qquad n = 64$$

Figure 2: An illustration of the square root law

This is called the *square root law* (or the $\sqrt{n}$-law) for the standard deviation. It is an extremely important result in probability and statistics. In Figure 2 an experimental demonstration of the $\sqrt{n}$-law is given. For each of the values $n = 1$, 4, 16 and 64, one hundred random outcomes of the so-called sample mean $\frac{1}{n}\sum_{k=1}^{n} X_k$ are given for the case that the X_k have a same probability distribution with expected value 0 and standard deviation 1 (this distribution is the standard normal distribution, which will be discussed in section 3.2). The observed outcomes are determined by computer simulation. You see from the figure that the bandwidths within which the simulated outcomes lie are indeed reduced by an factor of about 2 when the sample sizes increase by a factor of 4.

The $\sqrt{n}$-law is sometimes called the De Moivre's equation, after Abraham de Moivre (1667–1754).[11] This formula had an immediate

---

[11]The French-born Abraham de Moivre was the leading probabilist of the eighteenth century and lived most of his life in England. The protestant De Moivre left France in 1688 to escape religious persecution. He was a good friend of Isaac

impact on methods used to inspect gold coins struck at the London Mint. The standard gold weight, per coin, was 128 grains (this was equal to 0.0648 gram), and the allowable deviation from this standard was $\frac{1}{400}$ of that amount, or 0.32 grains. A test case of 100 coins was periodically performed on coins struck, their total weight then being compared with the standard weight of 100 coins. The gold used in the striking of coins was the property of the king, who sent inspectors to discourage minting mischief. The royal watch dogs had traditionally allowed a deviation of $100 \times 0.32 = 32$ grains in the weight of 100 inspected coins. Directly after De Moivre's publication of the square root formula, the allowable deviation in the weight of 100 coins was changed to $\sqrt{100} \times 0.32 = 3.2$ grains; alas for the English monarchy, previous ignorance of the square root formula had cost them a fortune in gold.

The square root law has many applications, providing explanation, for example, for why city or hospital size is important for measuring crime statistics or death rates after surgery. Small hospitals, for example, are more likely than large ones to appear at the top or bottom of ranking lists. This makes sense if you consider that, when tossing a fair coin, the probability that more than 70%, or less than 30%, of the tosses will turn up heads is much larger for 10 coin tosses, than for 100. The smaller the numbers, the larger the chance fluctuations!

Example 2.14. 'Unders and Overs' is a popular game formerly played during open house events at American schools, for the purpose of adding money to the school coffers. The game is played with two dice and a playing board divided into three sections: 'Under 7', '7', and 'Over 7'. The two dice are rolled, and players place chips on one or more of the three sections. Chips may be placed on the game board for 1 dollar apiece. For every chip placed in the 'Under 7' section, the payoff is 2 dollars if the total number of points rolled with the dice is less than 7. The payoff is the same for every chip in the 'Over 7' section if the total number of points is higher than 7.

Newton and supported himself by calculating odds for gamblers and insurers and by giving private lessons to students.

The payoff is 5 dollars for each chip placed on '7' if the total number of points is 7. A popular strategy is to place 1 chip on each of the three sections. Suppose that 500 rounds of the game are played, using this strategy. In each round there is a single player. What are the expected value and standard deviation of the net amount taken in by the school as a result of the 500 bets?

Solution. Let the random variable X be the net profit of the school in a single play of the game. The random variable X can take on the two values \$1 and $-\$2$. The net profit is $3 - 5 = -2$ if the sum of the dice is 7 and is $3 - 2 = 1$ otherwise. Using the results of Example 2.10, you find $P(X = -2) = \frac{6}{36}$ and $P(X = 1) = 1 - P(X = -2) = \frac{30}{36}$. This gives

$$E(X) = -2 \times \frac{6}{36} + 1 \times \frac{30}{36} = \frac{1}{2}.$$

To get $\sigma(X)$, use the formula $\sigma^2(X) = E(X^2) - \big(E(X)\big)^2$ and calculate $E(X^2) = 4 \times \frac{6}{36} + 1 \times \frac{30}{36} = \frac{3}{2}$. Thus $\sigma^2(X) = \frac{3}{2} - (\frac{1}{2})^2 = \frac{5}{4}$ and so

$$\sigma(X) = \frac{1}{2}\sqrt{5}.$$

The total net profit of the school is $X_1 + \cdots + X_{500}$ dollars, where X_i is the net profit of the school in the ith round. The random variables $X_1, \ldots, X_{500}$ are each distributed as X and are independent of each other. Using the linearity property of expectation,

$$E(X_1 + \cdots + X_{500}) = 500 \times \frac{1}{2} = 250 \text{ dollars.}$$

By the $\sqrt{n}$-law for the standard deviation,

$$\sigma(X_1 + \cdots + X_{500}) = \frac{1}{2}\sqrt{5} \times \sqrt{500} = 25 \text{ dollars.}$$

Problem 2.31. Consider again Problem 2.29. What are the expected value and the standard deviation of X? (answer: 4.472 and 1.404)

Problem 2.32. Investment A has a 0.8 probability of a \$2 000 profit and a 0.2 probability of a \$3 000 loss. Investment B has a 0.2 probability of a \$5 000 profit and a 0.8 probability of a zero profit. Verify that both investments have the same expected value and the same standard deviation for the net profit. (answer: expected value is $1 000 and standard deviation is $2 000)

Problem 2.33. Verify $\text{var}(aX + b) = a^2\text{var}(X)$ for any constants a and b.

Problem 2.34. Let the random variable X have the so-called *Bernoulli distribution* (named after the Swiss mathematician Jakob Bernoulli (1654–1705), the originator of the law of large numbers):

$$P(X = 1) = p \text{ and } P(X = 0) = 1 - p.$$

Verify that $E(X) = p$ and $\sigma(X) = \sqrt{p(1 - p)}$.

Problem 2.35. Six cards are taken from a deck: two kings and four aces. The six cards are thoroughly shuffled after which the two top cards are revealed. If both cards are aces, you win $1.25; otherwise, you lose $1. Is this bet favorable to you? (answer: no, your expected loss is $0.10)

Problem 2.36. A bowl has 10 white and 2 red balls. You pick m balls at random, where m can be chosen at your discretion. If each ball picked is white, you win $$m$; otherwise, you win nothing. What value of m maximizes your expected winnings? (answer: $m = 4$, expected winnings is $1.70)

Problem 2.37. In a round of a roulette game, you win $1 with probability $\frac{18}{37}$ or you lose $1 with probability $\frac{19}{37}$. What are the expected value and the standard deviation of your net loss in 100 rounds? (answer: $2.70 and $10.00)

Appendix: Proofs for expected value and standard deviation

This appendix aims to give you some insight into the proof of the properties of the expected value and the variance given in section 2.6. This will be done for the special case that X and Y are discrete random variables that can take on only a finite number of values. Let I be the set of possible values of X and J be the set of possible values of Y. For the moment, you are asked to take for granted the following basic result that will be proved at the end of the appendix: for any function $g(x,y)$, the expected value of the random variable $g(X,Y)$ is given by

$$E\big(g(X,Y)\big) = \sum_{x\in I}\sum_{y\in J} g(x,y)P(X = x \text{ and } Y = y).$$

A double sum must be read as follows

$$\sum_{i=1}^{n}\sum_{j=1}^{m} a_{ij} = \sum_{i=1}^{n}(a_{i1} + \cdots + a_{im}).$$

You can always interchange the order of summation when there are finitely many terms:

$$\sum_{i=1}^{n}\sum_{j=1}^{m} a_{ij} = \sum_{j=1}^{m}\sum_{i=1}^{n} a_{ij}.$$

The following properties can be easily proved using the above basic result:

Property 1. $E(aX + bY) = aE(X) + bE(Y)$ for any constants a and b.

Property 2. $E(XY) = E(X)E(Y)$ if X and Y are independent of each other.

Property 3. $\text{var}(aX + bY) = a^2\text{var}(X) + b^2\text{var}(Y)$ for any constants a and b if X and Y are independent of each other.

Proof of Property 1. Using the basic result for $E(g(X, Y))$ for $g(x, y) = ax + by$, you get that $E(aX + bY)$ is equal to

$$\sum_{x\in I}\sum_{y\in J}(ax + by)P(X = x \text{ and } Y = y)$$

$$= \sum_{x\in I}\sum_{y\in J}ax\,P(X = x \text{ and } Y = y) + \sum_{x\in I}\sum_{y\in J}by\,P(X = x \text{ and } Y = y)$$

$$= a\sum_{x\in I}x\sum_{y\in J}P(X = x \text{ and } Y = y) + b\sum_{y\in J}y\sum_{x\in I}P(X = x \text{ and } Y = y),$$

where the order of summation is interchanged in the second term of the last equation. Next you use the formula

$$P(X = x) = \sum_{y\in J}P(X = x \text{ and } Y = y).$$

This formula is a direct consequence of Axiom 3 in section 2.1. A similar formula applies to $P(Y = y)$. This gives

$$E(aX+bY) = a\sum_{x\in I}xP(X = x)+b\sum_{y\in J}yP(Y = y) = aE(X)+bE(Y).$$

Proof of Property 2. The definition of independent random variables X and Y is $P(X = x \text{ and } Y = y) = P(X = x)P(Y = y)$ for all possible values x and y. Next, by applying the basic result for $E(g(X, Y))$ with $g(x, y) = xy$, you find that $E(XY)$ is equal to

$$\sum_{x\in I}\sum_{y\in J}xyP(X = x \text{ and } Y = y) = \sum_{x\in I}\sum_{y\in J}xyP(X = x)P(Y = y)$$

$$= \sum_{x\in I}xP(X = x)\sum_{y\in J}yP(Y = y) = E(X)E(Y).$$

Proof of Property 3. For ease of notation, write $E(X)$ as μ_X and $E(Y)$ as μ_Y. Using the alternative definition $\text{var}(V) = E(V^2) - \mu^2$ for the variance of a random variable V with expected value μ and using Property 1, you get

$$\text{var}(aX + bY) = E((aX + bY)^2) - (E(aX + bY))^2$$
$$= a^2E(X^2) + 2abE(XY) + b^2E(Y^2) - (a\mu_X + b\mu_Y)^2.$$

Next you use the independence of X and Y. This gives $E(XY) = E(X)E(Y)$, by Property 2, and so var$(aX + bY)$ is equal to

$$a^2 E(X^2) + 2ab\mu_X\mu_Y + b^2 E(Y^2) - a^2\mu_X^2 - 2ab\mu_X\mu_Y - b^2\mu_Y^2$$
$$= a^2[E(X^2) - \mu_X^2] + b^2[E(Y^2) - \mu_Y^2] = a^2\text{var}(X) + b^2\text{var}(Y).$$

To conclude, the basic result $E\big(g(X,Y)\big) = \sum_{(x,y)} g(x,y)P(X = x$ and $Y = y)$ is proved. The proof is very simple. Let $Z = g(X,Y)$, then $\sum_{(x,y)} g(x,y)P(X = x$ and $Y = y)$ is equal to

$$\sum_z \left[\sum_{(x,y):g(x,y)=z} g(x,y)P(X = x \text{ and } Y = y) \right]$$
$$= \sum_z z \sum_{(x,y):g(x,y)=z} P(X = x \text{ and } Y = y) = \sum_z zP(Z = z)$$
$$= E(Z) = E\big(g(X,Y)\big).$$

Taking $Y = X$ and $g(x,y) = g(x)$, this result proves the substitution formula in section 2.6 as special case.

Further Reading

Probability: A Lively Introduction by Henk Tijms, Cambridge University Press, 2017.

Chapter 3

Useful Probability Distributions with Applications

This chapter introduces you to two important discrete probability distributions and to two important continuous probability distributions. The discrete distributions are the binomial and the Poisson distributions, while the two continuous distributions are the normal and the exponential distributions. Insight is given to the practical relevance of these distributions.

3.1 The binomial and Poisson probability distributions

A random variable X with $0, 1, \ldots, n$ as possible values is said to have a *binomial distribution* with parameters n and p if

$$P(X = k) = \binom{n}{k} p^k (1 - p)^{n-k} \quad \text{for } k = 0, 1, \ldots, n,$$

where $\binom{n}{k}$ is the binomial coefficient. This distribution arises in probability problems that can be formulated within the framework of a sequence of physically independent trials, where each trial has the two possible outcomes 'success' (S) and 'failure' (F). The outcome success occurs with probability p and the outcome failure with probability $1 - p$. The random variable X defined as the total number of successes in n trials has a binomial distribution. This result is easily derived. The probability that a pre-specified sequence of k successes and $n - k$ failures will occur is $p^k (1 - p)^{n-k}$; for example, for $n = 5$ and $k = 3$, the sequence $SSMSM$ will occur with probability $p \times p \times (1 - p) \times p \times (1 - p) = p^3(1 - p)^2$. The total number of possible sequences with k successes and $n - k$ failures is $\binom{n}{k}$, since the binomial coefficient $\binom{n}{k}$ is the total number of ways to choose k different positions from n available positions, see section 1.1 in chapter 1. The expected value and standard deviation of X are given by

$$E(X) = np \text{ and } \sigma(X) = \sqrt{np(1 - p)}.$$

In order to derive these formulas, write X as $X = I_1 + \cdots + I_n$, where the random variable I_k is 1 if the kth trial is a success and I_k is 0 otherwise. The Bernoulli variable I_k has $E(I_k) = p$ and $\text{var}(I_k) = p(1 - p)$, see Problem 2.34. Applying the linearity property for expectation and the $\sqrt{n}$-law for the standard deviation (the I_k's are independent of each other), you get

$$E\left(\sum_{k=1}^{n} I_k\right) = \sum_{k=1}^{n} E(I_k) = np \text{ and } \sigma\left(\sum_{k=1}^{n} I_k\right) = \sqrt{p(1 - p)} \times \sqrt{n}.$$

A random variable X with $0, 1, \ldots$ as possible values is said to have a *Poisson distribution* with parameter $\lambda > 0$ if

$$P(X = k) = e^{-\lambda} \frac{\lambda^k}{k!} \quad \text{for } k = 0, 1, \ldots,$$

where $e = 2.71828\ldots$ is the Euler number. The expected value and the standard deviation of X are

$$E(X) = \lambda \text{ and } \sigma(X) = \sqrt{\lambda}.$$

These formulas follow directly from the results at the end of the appendix of chapter 1. These results give that $E(X) = \lambda$ and $E(X(X - 1)) = \lambda^2$, and so $E(X^2) = \lambda^2 + \lambda$ and $\sigma^2(X) = (\lambda^2 + \lambda) - \lambda^2 = \lambda$, as was to be verified.

The binomial distribution can be used to solve the famous *problem of points*. In 1654 this problem was posed to Pascal and Fermat by the compulsory gambler Chevalier de Méré. Mathematics historians believe that the Chevalier posed the following problem: "Two players play a chance game of three points and each player has staked 32 pistols. How should the sum be divided if they break off prematurely when one player has two points and the other player has one point?" A similar problem was earlier posed by the Italian mathematician Luca Pacioli in 1494 and led to heated discussions among Italian mathematicians in the 16th century, but none of them could come up with a satisfactory answer. The starting insight for Pascal and Fermat was that what is important is not so much the number of points each player has won yet, but the ultimate win probabilities of the players if the game were to continue at the point of stopping. The stakes should be divided in proportion to these win probabilities. Today the solution to the problem is obvious, but it was not at all obvious how to solve the problem in a time that the theory of probability was at an embryonic stage. The next example analyzes the problem of points in a modern outfit.

Example 3.1. In the World Series Baseball, the final two teams play a series consisting of no more than seven games until one of the teams has won four games. The winner takes all of the prize money of $1 000 000. In one such a final, two teams are pitted against other and the stronger team will win any given game with a probability of 0.55. Unexpectedly, the competition must be suspended when the weaker team leads two games to one. How should the prize money be divided if the remaining games cannot be played?

Solution. At the point of stopping, the weaker team is 2 points away from the required 4 points and the stronger team 3 points. In the actual game at most $2 + 3 - 1 = 4$ more matches would be needed to declare a winner. A trick to solve the problem is to imagine that four additional matches would be played. The probability of the weaker team being the ultimate winner if the original game was to be continued is the same as the probability that the weaker team would win two or more matches in four additional matches (explain!). The latter probability is equal to the binomial probability

$$\sum_{k=2}^{4} \binom{4}{k} 0.45^k \, 0.55^{4-k} = 0.609019.$$

The weaker team should receive $609 019 and the stronger team $390 981.

A less famous but still interesting problem from the history of probability is the Newton–Pepys problem. Isaac Newton was not much interested in probability. Nevertheless Newton solved the following dice problem brought to him by Samuel Pepys who was a president of the Royal Society of London and apparently a gambling man. Which game is more likely to win: at least one six in one throw of six dice, at least two sixes in one throw of twelve dice, or at least three sixes in one throw of eighteen dice? What do you think? Pepys believed that the last option was the most favorable one.

Physical interpretation of the Poisson distribution

The Poisson distribution is a good approximation to the probability distribution of the total number of successes in a *very large* number of independent trials each having a *very small* probability of success. This is easily seen for the probability of zero successes. In n physically independent trials each having a probability p of success, the probability of no success at all is

$$(1 - p) \times (1 - p) \times \cdots \times (1 - p) = (1 - p)^n.$$

Section 1.2 of chapter 1 gives the useful approximation

$$e^{-x} \approx 1 - x \text{ for } x \text{ close to } 0.$$

By this approximation, $(1 - p)^n$ can be approximated by $(e^{-p})^n = e^{-np}$ if p is very small. Therefore the probability of no success in n independent trials each having a very small success probability p is approximately equal to $e^{-\lambda}$ with $\lambda = np$. More generally, it can be proved that the binomial probability $\binom{n}{k}p^k(1 - p)^{n-k}$ of getting exactly k successes in n independent trials tends to $e^{-\lambda}\lambda^k/k!$ as n gets very large and p very small such that np tends to a constant $\lambda > 0$, see the appendix in chapter 1.

A very important observation is that only the product value $\lambda = np$ is relevant for the Poisson approximation to the binomial distribution with parameters n and p. You do not need to know the particular values of the number of trials and the success probability. It is enough to know what the expected (or average) value of the total number of successes is. This is an extremely useful property when it comes to practical applications. The physical background of the Poisson distribution, as a distribution of the total number of successes in a large number of trials each having a small probability of success, explains why this distribution has so many practical applications: the annual number of damage claims at insurance companies, the annual number of severe traffic accidents in a given region, the annual number of stolen credit cards, the annual number of fatal shark bites worldwide, etc. The mathematical derivation of the Poisson distribution assumes that the trials are physically independent of each other, but, in many practical situations, the Poisson distribution also appears to give good approximations when there is a 'weak' dependence between the outcomes of the trials. This Poisson heuristic is especially useful for quickly arriving at good approximated results in problems for which it would otherwise be difficult to find exact solutions, see chapter 4 for examples.

Bombs over London in World War II

A famous application of the Poisson model is the analysis of the distribution of hits of flying bombs (V-1 and V-2 missiles) in London during the second World War. The British authorities were anxious to know if these weapons could be accurately aimed at a particular target, or whether they were landing at random. If the missiles were in fact only randomly targeted, the British could simply disperse important installations to decrease the likelihood of their being hit. An area of 36 square kilometers in South London was divided into 576 regions of 250 meter wide by 250 meter long, and the number of hits in each region was determined. The 576 regions were struck by 535 bombs and so the average number of hits per region was 0.9288. There were 229 regions with zero hits, 211 regions with one hit, 93 regions with two hits, 35 regions with three hits, 7 regions with four hits, 1 region with five hits, and 0 regions with six or more hits. If the number of hits in a region would have a Poisson distribution with expected value 0.9288, you would expect $576 \times e^{-0.9288} 0.9288^k/k!$ regions with exactly k hits, that is, 227.5 regions with zero hits, 211.3 regions with one hit, 98.1 regions with two hits, 30.4 regions with three hits, 7.1 regions with four hits, and 1.5 regions with five or more hits. You see that the observed relative frequencies of the number of hits are each very close to these theoretical relative frequencies. It could be concluded that the distribution of hits in the area was much like the distribution of hits when each of the many flying bombs was to fall on any of the equally sized regions with the same small probability, independently of the other flying bombs. The analysis convinced the British military that the bombs struck at random and had no advanced aiming ability.

The z-score test

A practically useful characteristic of the Poisson distribution is that the probability of a value more than three standard deviations removed from the expected value is very small (10^{-3} or smaller) when the expected value λ is sufficiently large. A rule of thumb is $\lambda \geq 25$. This characteristic is very useful for judging the value of all sorts of statistical facts reported in the media. In order to judge how exceptional a certain random outcome is, you measure how many standard deviations the outcome is removed from the expected value. This is called the *z-score test* in statistics. For example, suppose that in a given year the number of break-ins occurring in a given area increases more than 15% from an average of 64 break-ins per year to 75 break-ins. This is no reason to demand the resignation of the police officer, because the increase can be explained as a chance fluctuation (the value 75 is $11/\sqrt{64} = 1.38$ standard deviations above the expected value; the probability of this occurring is not negligible and is about 10%).

For a binomially distributed random variable X with parameters n and p it is also true that almost all probability mass from the distribution lies within three standard deviations of the expected value when $np(1-p)$ is sufficiently large. A rule of thumb for this is $np(1-p) > 20$. A beer brewery once made brilliant use of this. In a television advertisement spot broadcast during the American Super Bowl final, 100 beer drinkers were asked to do a blind taste test comparing beer brewed by the sponsored brewery, and beer brewed by a competitor. The brilliance of the stunt is that the 100 beer drinkers invited to participate were regular drinkers of the brand made by the competitor. In those days, all brands of American

Table 1: Binomial and Poisson probabilities

k	0	1	2	3	4	5	6
bin	0.2537	0.3484	0.2388	0.1089	0.0372	0.0101	0.0023
Poi	0.2541	0.3481	0.2385	0.1089	0.0373	0.0102	0.0023

beer tasted more or less the same, and most drinkers weren't able to distinguish between brands. The marketers of the sponsored beer could therefore be pretty sure that more than 35% of the participants in the stunt would prefer the sponsored beer over their regular beer (the binomial distribution with $n = 100$ and $p = 0.5$ has 99.8% of the probability mass above the value of 35; the z-score for 35 beer drinkers is $(35 - 50)/5 = -3$). This did, in fact, occur, and made quite an impression on the television audience.

Example 3.2. There are 500 people present at a gathering. For the fun of it, the organizers have decided that all of those whose birthday is that day will receive a present. How many presents should the organization procure in order to ensure a less than 1% probability of having too few presents?

Solution. Let the random variable X represent the number of individuals with a birthday on the day of the gathering. Leap year day, February 29, is discounted, and apart from that, it is assumed that every day of the year is equally likely as birthday. The distribution of X can then be modeled by a binomial distribution with parameters $n = 500$ and $p = \frac{1}{365}$. Calculations reveal that $k = 5$ suffices in order to have $P(X > k) < 0.01$. For $k = 5$, $P(X > k) = 0.0029$ and so five presents suffice. In this example, n is large and p is small such that the binomial distribution of X can be nicely approximated by a Poisson distribution with expected value $\lambda = np = \frac{500}{365}$. For comparison, both for the binomial distribution and the Poisson distribution, Table 1 gives the probability that exactly k persons have a birthday on the day of the gathering for $k = 0, 1, \ldots, 6$.

Problem 3.1. A fair coin is to be tossed six times You win two dollars if heads appears exactly three times (the expected number) and you lose one dollar otherwise. Is this game advantageous to you? (answer: no, your win probability is $\frac{5}{16}$)

Problem 3.2. Daily Airlines flies from Amsterdam to London every day. The price of a ticket for this extremely popular flight route is $75. The aircraft has a passenger capacity of 150. The airline management has made it a policy to sell 157 tickets for this flight in order to protect themselves against no-show passengers. Experience has shown that the probability of a passenger being a no-show is equal to 0.08. The booked passengers act independently of each other. Specify the probability distribution of the number of no-shows on a flight. What is the probability that some passengers will have to be bumped from the flight? (answer: 0.0285)

Problem 3.3. Chuck-a-Luck is a carnival game of chance and is played with three dice. To play this game, the player chooses one number from the numbers $1, \ldots, 6$. The three dice are then rolled. If the player's number does not come up at all, the player loses 10 dollars. If the chosen number comes up one, two, or three times, the player wins $10, $20, or $30 respectively. What are the expected value and the standard deviation of the win for the house per wager? (answer: $0.787 and $11.13)

Problem 3.4. In a game called '26', a player chooses one number from the numbers $1, 2, \ldots, 6$ as point number. After this, the player rolls a collection of ten dice thirteen times in succession. If the player's point number comes up 26 times or more, the player receives five times the amount staked on the game; otherwise, the player loses the stake. Is this game to the player's advantage? (answer: no, the player's win probability is 0.1820)

Problem 3.5. In an ESP-experiment a medium has to guess the correct symbol on each of 250 Zener cards. Each card has one of the five possible Zener symbols on it and each of the symbols is equally likely to appear. The medium will get $100 000 dollars if he gives 82 or more correct answers. This was the offer the famous skeptic James Randi once made to a self-declared clairvoyant who accepted the offer but failed hopelessly. Can you give a quick assessment of the probability that the medium would have to be paid out? (answer:

the z-score is $32/\sqrt{40} \approx 5.06$ for random guessing)

Problem 3.6. What is the probability of the jackpot falling in lotto 6/45 when 1 million tickets are filled in with random picks? (answer: 0.1155)

Problem 3.7. In a coastal area, the average number of serious hurricanes is 3.1 per year. What is an appropriate probability model to calculate the probability of a total of more than 5 serious hurricanes in the next year? What is a good estimate for this probability? (answer: 0.0943)

Problem 3.8. The low earth orbit contains many pieces of space debris. It is estimated that an orbiting space station will be hit by space debris beyond a critical size and speed on average once in 400 years. How do you estimate the probability that a newly launched space station will not be penetrated in the first 20 years? (answer: 0.951)

Problem 3.9. In a particular rural area, postal carriers are attacked by dogs 324 times per year on average. Last year there were 379 attacks. Is this exceptional? (answer: yes, the z-score is 3.1)

3.2 The normal and exponential probability densities

Many probabilistic situations are better described by a continuous random variable rather than a discrete random variable. Think of the annual rainfall in a certain area or the decay time of a radioactive particle. Calculations in probability and statistics are often greatly simplified by approximating the histogram of the probability mass function of a discrete random variable by a continuous curve. A histogram shows the probability mass function as a series of vertical bars. The histogram of the binomial distribution with parameters n and p can very well be approximated by the graph of the continuous function

$$f(x) = \frac{1}{\sigma\sqrt{2\pi}} \, e^{-\frac{1}{2}(x-\mu)^2/\sigma^2}$$

with $\mu = np$ and $\sigma = \sqrt{np(1-p)}$ if n is sufficiently large, say $np(1-p) \geq 20$. This function $f(x)$ is called the *normal density function* (or the *Gaussian density function*). Likewise the histogram of the Poisson distribution with parameter λ can be approximated by the graph of the normal density function $f(x)$ with $\mu = \lambda$ and $\sigma = \sqrt{\lambda}$ if λ is sufficiently large, say $\lambda \geq 25$. This is illustrated in Figure 3 for the binomial distribution with $n = 125$ and $p = \frac{1}{5}$ and the Poisson distribution with $\lambda = 25$.

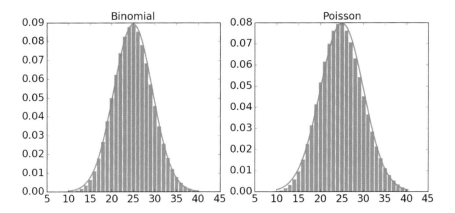

Figure 3: Normal approximation to binomial and Poisson probabilities

You have now arrived at the normal distribution, which is the most important continuous distribution. A continuous random variable X is said to have a *normal distribution* with parameters μ and $\sigma > 0$ if

$$P(X \leq x) = \frac{1}{\sigma\sqrt{2\pi}} \int_{-\infty}^{x} e^{-\frac{1}{2}(t-\mu)^2/\sigma^2} \, dt \quad \text{for } -\infty < x < \infty.$$

The notation $N(\mu, \sigma^2)$ is often used for a normally distributed random variable X with parameters μ and σ.

The normal density function $f(x) = \frac{1}{\sigma\sqrt{2\pi}} e^{-\frac{1}{2}(x-\mu)^2/\sigma^2}$ is the derivative of the probability distribution function $F(x) = P(X \leq x)$. The parameters μ and σ of the normal density function are the expected value and the standard deviation of X, that is,

$$\mu = \int_{-\infty}^{\infty} x f(x) \, dx \quad \text{and} \quad \sigma^2 = \int_{-\infty}^{\infty} (x - \mu)^2 f(x) \, dx.$$

The derivation of these formulas is beyond the scope of this book. The following remarks are made. The normal density function $f(x)$ is maximal for $x = \mu$ and is symmetric around the point $x = \mu$. The point $x = \mu$ is also the median of the normal probability distribution.[12] About 68.3% of the probability mass of a normally distributed random variable with expected value μ and standard deviation σ is between the points $\mu - \sigma$ and $\mu + \sigma$, about 95.4% between $\mu - 2\sigma$ and $\mu + 2\sigma$, and about 99.7% between $\mu - 3\sigma$ and $\mu + 3\sigma$. These facts are displayed in Figure 4 and will be explained below after having introduced the standard normal distribution.

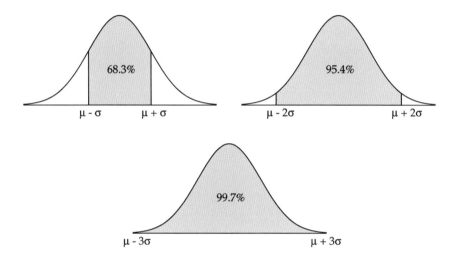

Figure 4: Characteristics of the normal density function

The normal distribution has the important characteristic that $aX + bY$ is normally distributed for any constants a and b if the random variables X and Y are normally distributed and independent of each other. The expected value μ and the standard deviation σ of $aX + bY$ are then equal to

$$\mu = aE(X) + bE(Y) \quad \text{and} \quad \sigma = \sqrt{a^2\sigma^2(X) + b^2\sigma^2(Y)}.$$

---

[12]The median of a continuous random variable is defined as a point such that the random variable has 50% of its probability mass left from that point and 50% of its probability mass right from that point.

It is also stated without proof that $aX + b$ is $N(a\mu + b, a^2\sigma^2)$ distributed if the random variable X is $N(\mu, \sigma^2)$ distributed.

The *standard normal distribution* is the normal distribution with expected value 0 and standard deviation 1. This distribution is usually denoted as the $N(0,1)$ distribution. For a standard normally distributed random variable Z, the notation

$$\Phi(z) = P(Z \leq z)$$

is used for the probability distribution function of Z. The function $\Phi(z)$ is given by the famous integral

$$\Phi(z) = \frac{1}{\sqrt{2\pi}} \int_{-\infty}^{z} e^{-\frac{1}{2}x^2} \, dx \quad \text{for any } z.$$

The numerical calculation of $\Phi(z)$ usually goes via $\Phi(z) = \frac{1}{2} + \frac{1}{2}\text{erf}(z/\sqrt{2})$ with $\text{erf}(x) = \frac{2}{\sqrt{\pi}} \int_0^x e^{-y^2} \, dy$, which is the Gauss error function.

If the random variable X has a normal distribution with expected value μ and standard deviation σ, then the *normalized* random variable

$$Z = \frac{X - \mu}{\sigma}$$

has a standard normal distribution. This is a very useful result for the calculation of the probabilities $P(X \leq x)$. Writing

$$P(X \leq x) = P\left(\frac{X - \mu}{\sigma} \leq \frac{x - \mu}{\sigma}\right),$$

you see that $P(X \leq x)$ can be calculated as

$$P(X \leq x) = \Phi\left(\frac{x - \mu}{\sigma}\right).$$

In particular, $P(X \leq \mu) = \Phi(0) = 0.5$. Using the formula $P(a < X \leq b) = P(X \leq b) - P(X \leq a)$, it follows that $P(a < X \leq b)$ can be calculated as

$$P(a < X \leq b) = \Phi\left(\frac{b - \mu}{\sigma}\right) - \Phi\left(\frac{a - \mu}{\sigma}\right) \quad \text{for any } a < b.$$

This result explains the numbers in Figure 4. As an example, an $N(\mu, \sigma^2)$ distributed random variable has about 95.4% of its probability mass between $\mu - 2\sigma$ and $\mu + 2\sigma$, since $\Phi(2) - \Phi(-2) = 0.9545$.

As an illustration of the normal distribution, the length of Northern European boys who are born after a gestational period between 38 and 42 weeks has a normal distribution with an expected value of 50.9 cm and a standard deviation of 2.4 cm at birth. How exceptional is it that a boy at birth has a length of 48 cm? A quick answer to this question can be given by using the z-score test: a length of 48 cm is $\frac{50.9 - 48}{2.4} = 1.2083$ standard deviations below the expected value and this is not exceptional. The undershoot probability $\Phi(-1.2083) = 0.1135$ corresponds to a z-score of -1.2083.

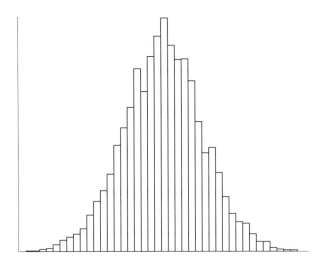

Figure 5: Histogram of height measurements

As said before, the normal distribution is the most important continuous distribution. Many stochastic situations in practice can be modeled with the help of the normal distribution. For example, the annual rainfall in a certain area, the cholesterol level of an adult male of a specific racial group, errors in physical measurements, the length of men in a certain age group, etc. Figure 5 displays a histogram of height measurements of a large number of men in a certain age group.

This histogram divides the range of values covered by the measurements into intervals of the same width, and shows the proportion of the measurements in each interval. You see that the histogram has the characteristic bell-shaped form of the graph of the normal density function. Making the width of the intervals smaller and smaller and the number of observations larger and larger, the graph of the histogram changes into the graph of a normal density function. The expected value and the standard deviation of this density function can be estimated from the observations. It is much simpler to perform calculations with the continuous normal density function than with the probability mass function underlying the histogram. Next the most famous theorem of probability and statistics is discussed.

The central limit theorem

An explanation can be given for the finding that many stochastic situations in practice can be modeled with the help of a normal distribution. If a random variable can be seen as the result of the sum of a large number of small independent random effects, then it is approximately normally distributed. Mathematically, this result is expressed by the *central limit theorem*, which can be considered as the most celebrated theorem in probability and statistics. This theorem can be formulated as follows:

if the random variables $X_1, X_2, \ldots, X_n$ are independent of each other and have each the same probability distribution with expected value μ and standard deviation σ, then the sum $X_1 + X_2 + \cdots + X_n$ has approximately a normal distribution with expected value $n\mu$ and standard deviation $\sigma\sqrt{n}$ if n is sufficiently large.

Alternatively, the central limit theorem can be formulated as: the sample mean $\frac{1}{n}(X_1 + X_2 + \cdots + X_n)$ has approximately a normal distribution with expected value μ and standard deviation $\frac{\sigma}{\sqrt{n}}$ if n is sufficiently large (use the fact that $E(aX) = aE(X)$ and $\sigma(aX) = a\sigma(X)$ for any constant $a > 0$). These results can be expressed in the following two mathematical formulas. For any number x,

$$P(X_1 + X_2 + \cdots + X_n \leq x) \approx \Phi \left(\frac{x - n\mu}{\sigma\sqrt{n}} \right) \quad \text{for large } n$$

$$P \left(\frac{X_1 + X_2 + \cdots + X_n}{n} \leq x \right) \approx \Phi \left(\frac{x - \mu}{\sigma/\sqrt{n}} \right) \quad \text{for large } n.$$

How large n should be depends on the shape of the probability distribution of the X_i; the more symmetric this distribution is, the sooner the normal approximation applies. The central limit theorem is extremely useful for both practical and theoretical purposes. To illustrate, consider Example 2.14 again. Using the fact that an $N(\alpha, \beta^2)$ distributed random variable has 95.4% of its probability mass between $\alpha - 2\beta$ and $\alpha + 2\beta$, there is a probability of about 95% that the net profit of the school after 500 bets will be between $250 - 2 \times 25 = 200$ dollars and $250 + 2 \times 25 = 300$ dollars.

The central limit theorem explains why the histogram of the probability mass function of a binomially distributed random variable with parameters n and p can be nicely approximated by the graph of a normal density with expected value np and standard deviation $\sqrt{np(1-p)}$ if n is sufficiently large. As you have seen before, a binomial random variable can be written as the sum $X_1 + \cdots + X_n$ of n independent random variables X_i with $P(X_i = 1) = p$ and $P(X_i = 0) = 1 - p$.

The central limit theorem has an interesting history. The first version of this theorem was postulated in 1738 by the French-born English mathematician Abraham de Moivre, who used the normal distribution to approximate the distribution of the number of heads resulting from many tosses of a fair coin. De Moivre's finding was far ahead of its time, and was nearly forgotten until the famous French mathematician Pierre Simon Laplace rescued it from obscurity in his monumental work *Théorie Analytique des Probabilités*, which was published in 1812. Laplace expanded De Moivre's finding by approximating the binomial distribution with the normal distribution. But as with De Moivre, Laplace's finding received little attention in his own time. It was not until the nineteenth century was at an end that the importance of the central limit theorem was discerned, when, in 1901, the Russian mathematician Aleksandr Lyapunov defined it in general terms and proved precisely how it worked mathematically. Nowadays, the central limit theorem is considered to be the unofficial sovereign of probability theory.

Example 3.3. For an expedition with a duration of one and a half years, a number of spare copies of a particular filter must be taken along. The filter will be used daily. The lifetime of the filter has a continuous probability distribution with an expected value of one week and a standard deviation of half a week. Upon failure a filter is replaced immediately by a new one. How many filters should be taken along with the expedition in order to ensure that there will be no shortage with a probability of at least 99%?

Solution. Suppose that n filters are taken along. The probability of no shortage during the expedition is $P(X_1 + \cdots + X_n > 78)$, where X_i is the lifetime of the ith filter. It is supposed that the lifetimes of the filters are independent of each other. Then, by the central limit theorem,

$$P(X_1 + \cdots + X_n > 78) = 1 - P(X_1 + \cdots + X_n \leq 78)$$
$$= 1 - P\left(\frac{X_1 + \cdots + X_n - n}{0.5\sqrt{n}} \leq \frac{78 - n}{0.5\sqrt{n}}\right) \approx 1 - \Phi\left(\frac{78 - n}{0.5\sqrt{n}}\right).$$

The requirement is that $1 - \Phi\big((78 - n)/(0.5\sqrt{n})\big) \geq 0.99$, and so you need the smallest value of n for which $\Phi\big((78 - n)/(0.5\sqrt{n})\big) \leq 0.01$. The solution of the equation $\Phi(x) = 0.01$ is $x = -2.326$ (the so-called 1% percentile[13]). Next you solve the equation

$$\frac{78 - z}{0.5\sqrt{z}} = -2.326.$$

The solution is $z = 88.97$. Thus 89 copies of the filter should be taken along.

Problem 3.10. The annual rainfall in Amsterdam has a normal distribution with an expected value of 799.5 mm and a standard

---

[13]For any $0 < p < 1$, the $100p\%$ percentile ξ_p of the standard normal distribution is defined as the unique solution to $\Phi(x) = p$. For example, $\xi_{0.95} = 1.645$ and $\xi_{0.99} = 2.326$.

deviation of 121.4 mm. What is the probability of having more than 1000 mm rainfall in Amsterdam next year? (answer: 0.0493)

Problem 3.11. Gestation periods of humans have a normal distribution with an expected value of 280 days and a standard deviation of 10 days. What is the percentage of births that are more than 15 days overdue? (answer: 0.0668)

Problem 3.12. The diameter of a 1 euro coin has a normal distribution with an expected value of 23.25 mm and a standard deviation of 0.10 mm. A vending machine accepts only 1 euro coins with a diameter between 22.90 mm and 23.60 mm. What is the probability that a 1 euro coin will not be accepted by the vending machine? (answer: 4.65×10^{-4})

Problem 3.13. The annual grain harvest in a certain area is normally distributed with an expected value of 15 000 tons and a standard deviation of 2 000 tons. In the past year the grain harvest was 21 500 tons. Is this exceptional? (answer: yes, the z-score is 3.25)

Problem 3.14. Somebody claims to have obtained 5 249 heads in 10 000 tosses of a fair coin. Do you believe this? (answer: no, the z-score is 5.0)

Problem 3.15. What is the standard deviation of the demand for a certain item if the demand has a normal distribution with an expected value of 100 and the probability of a demand exceeding 125 is 0.05? (answer: 15.2)

Problem 3.16. A stock return can be modeled by an $N(\mu, \sigma^2)$ distributed random variable. An investor believes that there is a 10% probability of a return below $80 and a 10% probability of a return above $120. What are the investor's estimates of μ and σ? (answer: $\mu = 100$ and $\sigma = 15.6$)

Problem 3.17. An insurance company has 20 000 policyholders. The amount claimed yearly by a policyholder has an expected value of $150 and a standard deviation of $750. Use the central limit theorem to get an approximation for the probability that the total amount claimed in the coming year will be larger than 3.3 million dollars. (answer: 0.0023)

Problem 3.18. A casino offers a game that will be won by the player with probability $\frac{18}{37}$ and by the casino with probability $\frac{19}{37}$. The player gets back twice the stake if the player wins; otherwise, the player loses the stake. What is the probability distribution of the net profit of the casino after 10 000 rounds with a single player betting each time one dollar? (answer: a normal distribution with an expected value of $270.27 and a standard deviation of $99.96)

The concept of probability density function[14]

What is the exact meaning of the concept of probability density function? This is a tricky and subtle concept when you hear it for the first time. Whereas a discrete random variable associates *positive* probabilities to its individual values, any individual value has probability *zero* for a continuous random variable. It is only meaningful to speak of the probability of a continuous random variable taking on a value in some interval. The most simple example of a continuous random variable is the choice of a *random number* from the interval $(0, 1)$ (think of throwing blindly a dart with an infinitely thin point on the interval $(0, 1)$). The probability that the randomly chosen number will take on a pre-specified value is zero. It makes only sense to speak of the probability of the randomly chosen number falling in a subinterval of $(0, 1)$. The probability of the random number falling in the subinterval is equal to the length of the subinterval and so each subinterval of the same length has the same probability of containing the random number. You can say that the probability mass associated with a randomly chosen number is smeared out over the interval $(0, 1)$ in such a way that the density is the same everywhere. This density is called the uniform (or homogeneous) density. In general, the probability mass of a continuous random variable is smeared out, as were it liquid mass, over the range of the possible values according

---

[14]The rest of section 3.2 can be skipped without loss of continuity.

to a specific density function. How do you express this mathematically? The answer to this question requires differential and integral calculus.

Let X be a *continuous* random variable. A nonnegative function $f(x)$ with $\int_{-\infty}^{\infty} f(x)\,dx = 1$ is said to be the *probability density function* of X if $f(x)$ is continuous with the possible exception of a finite number of points and

$$P(X \leq x) = \int_{-\infty}^{x} f(y)\,dy \quad \text{for all } x.$$

The number $f(x)$ is not a probability but a measure of how densely the probability mass of X is smeared out around the point x. To see this, note that $f(x)$ is the derivative of $P(X \leq x)$ and so, for small $\Delta x > 0$,

$$P(x < X \leq x + \Delta x) = P(X \leq x + \Delta x) - P(X \leq x) \approx f(x)\Delta x$$

for any continuity point x of $f(x)$.

Let R be the range of possible values of the continuous random variable X. Then, by the interpretation of $f(x)\Delta x$ for Δx very small, it is reasonable to define the expected value of X as

$$E(X) = \int_R x f(x)\,dx,$$

assuming that the integral is well-defined. For any function $g(x)$, the substitution formula states that

$$E[g(X)] = \int_R g(x)\,f(x)\,dx,$$

provided that the integral is well-defined.

Using the formula $P(a < X \leq b) = P(X \leq b) - P(X \leq a)$, integral calculus tells you that

$$P(a < X \leq b) = \int_a^b f(x)\,dx$$

for any constants a and b with $a < b$. The integral $\int_a^b f(x)\,dx$ gives the area under the graph of the density function $f(x)$ between the points a and b, and so this area represents the probability mass of X between the points a and b. For this probability mass, it does not matter whether the points a and b are included or not. Each individual point has probability mass zero for a continuous random variable X and so

$$P(a < X < b) = P(a < X \leq b) = P(a \leq X < b) = P(a \leq X \leq b).$$

The exponential probability density

Besides the normal density function, a very important probability density function is the *exponential density function* with parameter $\lambda > 0$:

$$f(x) = \lambda e^{-\lambda x} \quad \text{for } x \geq 0$$

and $f(x) = 0$ for $x < 0$. A continuous random variable with this density can only take on positive values. The exponential probability distribution is often used to model the time until the occurrence of a rare event (e.g., serious earthquake, the decay of a radioactive particle). Figure 6 gives the histogram of a large number of observations of the time until decay of a radioactive particle. An exponential density function can indeed be very well fitted to this histogram.

The probability distribution function $F(x) = P(X \leq x)$ of the random variable X with the density function $f(x) = \lambda e^{-\lambda x}$ is given by (verify!)

$$F(x) = \int_0^x f(y)\, dy = 1 - e^{-\lambda x} \quad \text{for } x \geq 0.$$

A well-known formula in integral calculus is

$$\int_0^\infty x^k e^{-\lambda x}\, dx = \frac{k!}{\lambda^{k+1}} \quad \text{for } k = 0, 1, \ldots \text{ and } \lambda > 0.$$

Using this formula, you find that the expected value and standard deviation of X are given by

$$E(X) = \int_0^\infty x f(x)\, dx = \frac{1}{\lambda}, \quad \sigma^2(X) = \int_0^\infty \left(x - \frac{1}{\lambda}\right)^2 f(x)\, dx = \frac{1}{\lambda^2}.$$

This means that the standard deviation of an exponentially distributed random variable is always equal to the expected value.

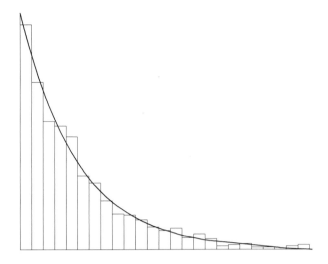

Figure 6: A histogram for decay times

A characteristic property of the exponential distribution is its *lack of memory*. That is, for any $s > 0$, the exponential random variable X satisfies

$$P(X > s + x \mid X > s) = P(X > x) \quad \text{for all } x > 0.$$

In other words, imagining that X represents the lifetime of an item, the residual life of the item has the same exponential distribution as the original lifetime, regardless of how long the item has been already in use ('used is as good as new'). The proof of the memoryless property is very simple. Using the formulas $P(A \mid B) = P(A \text{ and } B)/P(B)$ and $P(X > v) = e^{-\lambda v}$ for all $v > 0$, you find for any $s > 0$ that

$$P(X > s + x \mid X > s) = \frac{P(X > s + x \text{ and } X > s)}{P(X > s)} = \frac{P(X > s + x)}{P(X > s)}$$

$$= \frac{e^{-\lambda(s+x)}}{e^{-\lambda s}} = e^{-\lambda x} \quad \text{for all } x > 0.$$

The continuous exponential distribution is closely related to the discrete Poisson distribution. Suppose that radioactive material emits particles one at a time, where the interoccurrence times are independent of each other and each have a same exponential density function. Letting λ be the average number of emissions per unit time, then the number of emissions in any time interval of length t has a Poisson distribution with expected value λt and is independent of the number of emissions that occurred before that time interval. This explains why a random process in which the times between the occurrences of consecutive events are independent of each other and each have the same exponential density function is called a *Poisson process*. By its memoryless property, the Poisson process is one of the most important random processes in probability theory. It is used to model random processes in many areas such as inventory control, maintenance and reliability, and telecommunications.

Example 3.4. In a traditional match between two university soccer teams the lengths of time between goals are independent of each other and have an exponential distribution with an expected value of 30 minutes. The playing time of the match is 90 minutes. What is the probability of having three or more goals during the match? What is the probability that exactly two goals will be scored in the first half of the match and exactly one goal in the second half?

Solution. Goals are scored at a rate of $\lambda = \frac{1}{30}$ per minute. The number of goals scored during the match has a Poisson distribution with an expected value of $\lambda \times 90 = 3$. Therefore the probability of having three or more goals during the match is given by

$$1 - \sum_{k=0}^{2} e^{-3} \frac{3^k}{k!} = 0.5768.$$

By the memoryless property of the exponential distribution, the number of goals scored in the first half of the match and the number of goals scored in the second half of the match are independent of each other and have each a Poisson distribution with an expected value of $\lambda \times 45 = 1.5$. Thus the probability that exactly two goals will be scored in the first half of the match and exactly one goal in the second half is given by

$$e^{-1.5} \frac{1.5^2}{2!} \times e^{-1.5} 1.5 = 0.0840.$$

Problem 3.19. Taxis arrive at a stand, one at a time, with independent interarrival times that are exponentially distributed with an expected value of 10 minutes. What is the conditional probability that you will have to wait more than 7 minutes until the next taxi arrives given that the last taxi arrived 3 minutes ago? What is this probability if the last taxi arrived 12 minutes ago? (answer: 0.4966 and 0.4966)

Problem 3.20. A satellite has a lifetime that is exponentially distributed with an expected value of 15 years. What are the expected value and the standard deviation of the residual lifetime of the satellite when it is in use for already 12 years? (answer: both are 15 years)

Problem 3.21. In a hospital five babies are born per 24 hours on average. It is reasonable to model the times between the arrivals of the babies by exponentially distributed random variables that are independent of each other and have each an expected value of $\frac{24}{5}$ hours. What is the probability that more than two babies will be born between twelve o'clock midnight and six o'clock in the morning? (answer: 0.1315)

3.3 The chi-square test

The chi-square test (χ^2 test) is one of the most useful statistical tests. It is used to test whether data were generated from a particular probability distribution. The test can also be used to judge whether data have been manipulated to make the observed frequencies closer to the expected ones.

Suppose you want to find out whether the probability mass function $p_1, \ldots, p_r$ fits a random sample of observations obtained for a repeatable chance experiment with a finite number of possible outcomes $O_1, \ldots, O_r$. To introduce the chi-square test, denote by the random variable N_j the number of times that outcome O_j will appear in n physically independent repetitions of the chance experiment in which outcome O_j occurs with probability p_j. The random variable N_j has a binomial distribution with parameters n and p_j, and so the expected value of N_j is np_j. By the principle of least squares, it is reasonable to consider a test statistic of the form $\sum_{j=1}^{r} w_j(N_j - np_j)^2$ for appropriately chosen weights w_j. It turns out that the choice $w_j = \frac{1}{np_j}$ yields a statistic with a tractable distribution. Thus the so-called chi-square statistic is defined by

$$D = \sum_{j=1}^{r} \frac{(N_j - np_j)^2}{np_j}.$$

The exact probability distribution of the statistic D is difficult to compute. Fortunately, the discrete probability distribution of D can be very accurately approximated by a well-studied continuous probability distribution when np_j is sufficiently large for all j, say $np_j \geq 5$ for all j (in order to achieve this, it might be necessary to pool some data groups). Then,

$$P(D \leq x) \approx P(\chi_{r-1}^2 \leq x) \quad \text{for } x \geq 0,$$

where the continuous random variable χ_{r-1}^2 is distributed as the sum of the squares of $r-1$ independent $N(0,1)$ distributed random variables. The probability distribution of χ_{r-1}^2 is called the chi-square distribution with $r-1$ degrees of freedom. Its expected value is $E(\chi_{r-1}^2) = r - 1$. It should be pointed out that the above approximation for the chi-square statistic D assumes that the probabilities p_j are not estimated from the data but are known beforehand; if you have to estimate one or more parameters to get the probabilities p_j, you must lower the number of degrees of freedom of the chi-square distribution by one for every parameter estimated from the data.

How do you apply the chi-square test in practice? Using the data that you have obtained for the chance experiment in question, you calculate what numerical value d the test statistic D takes on for these data. The (subjective) judgment whether the probability mass function $p_1, \ldots, p_r$ fits the data depends on the value of the probability $P(D \leq d)$. All this will be illustrated in the following two examples.

Example 3.5. Somebody claims to have rolled a fair die 1 200 times and to have found that the outcomes 1, 2, 3, 4, 5, and 6 occurred 196, 202, 199, 198, 202, and 203 times. Do you believe these results?

Solution. The reported frequencies are very close to the expected frequencies. Taking into consideration that, for each j, the number of rolls with outcome j has an expected value of $1\,200 \times \frac{1}{6} = 200$ and a standard deviation of $\sqrt{1\,200 \times (1/6) \times (5/6)} = 12.91$, you should be suspicious about the reported results. You can substantiate this with the chi-square test. For the reported frequencies, the chi-square statistic D takes on the value

$$\frac{1}{200}\big[(196 - 200)^2 + (202 - 200)^2 + (199 - 200)^2 + (198 - 200)^2$$
$$+ (202 - 200)^2 + (203 - 200)^2\big] = 0.19.$$

The value 0.19 lies far below the expected value 5 of the chi-square distribution with $6 - 1 = 5$ degrees of freedom. The probability $P(D \leq 0.19)$ is approximated by $P(\chi_5^2 \leq 0.19) = 0.00078$. This is an excellent approximation (the simulated value of $P(D \leq 0.19)$ is 0.00083 after 4 million simulation runs). The very small probability for the test statistic indicates that the data are indeed most likely fabricated.

Example 3.6. A total of 64 matches were played during the World Cup soccer 2010 in South Africa. The number of goals per match was distributed as follows. There were 7 matches with zero goals, 17 matches with 1 goal, 13 matches with two goals, 14 matches with three goals, 7 matches with four goals, 5 matches with five goals, and 1 match with seven goals. Does a Poisson distribution fit closely these data?

Solution. In this example you must first estimate the parameter λ of the hypothesized Poisson distribution. This parameter is estimated as

$$\frac{1}{64}\big(17 \times 1 + 13 \times 2 + 14 \times 3 + 7 \times 4 + 5 \times 5 + 0 \times 6 + 1 \times 7\big) = \frac{145}{64}.$$

In order to satisfy the requirement that each data group should have an expected size of at least 5, the matches with 5 or more goals are aggregated, and so six data groups are considered. If a Poisson distribution with expected value $\lambda = \frac{145}{64}$ applies, then the expected number of matches with exactly j goals is $64 \times e^{-\lambda}\lambda^j/j!$ for

$j = 0, 1, \ldots, 4$ and the expected number of matches with 5 or more goals is $64 \times (1 - \sum_{j=0}^{4} e^{-\lambda} \lambda^j / j!)$. These expected numbers have the respective values 6.641, 15.046, 17.044, 12.872, 7.291, and 5.106. Thus the value of the chi-square test statistic D is given by

$$d = \frac{(7 - 6.641)^2}{6.641} + \frac{(17 - 15.046)^2}{15.046} + \frac{(13 - 17.044)^2}{17.044} + \frac{(14 - 12.872)^2}{12.872}$$
$$+ \frac{(7 - 7.291)^2}{7.291} + \frac{(6 - 5.106)^2}{5.106} = 1.500.$$

Since the parameter λ of the Poisson distribution has been estimated from the data, the test statistic D has approximately a chi-square distribution with $6 - 1 - 1 = 4$ degrees of freedom. The probability $P(\chi_4^2 \geq 1.500) = 0.827$. Thus the Poisson distribution gives an excellent fit to the data.

Problem 3.22. In a classical study on the distribution of 196 soldiers kicked to death by horses among 14 Prussian cavalry corps over the 20 years from 1875 to 1894, the data are as follows. In 144 corps-years no deaths occurred, 91 corps-years had one death, 32 corps-years had two deaths, 11 corps-years had three deaths, and 2 corps-years had four deaths. Does a Poisson distribution fit the data? (answer: yes, $P(\chi_2^2 \geq 1.952) = 0.377$)[15]

Problem 3.23. In a famous physics experiment performed by Rutherford, Chadwick and Ellis in 1920, the number of α-particles emitted by a piece of radioactive material were counted during 2 608 time intervals of each 7.5 seconds. Denoting by O_j denotes the number of intervals with exactly j particles, the observed data are $O_0 = 57$, $O_1 = 203$, $O_2 = 383$, $O_3 = 525$, $O_4 = 532$, $O_5 = 408$, $O_6 = 273$, $O_7 = 139$, $O_8 = 45$, $O_9 = 27$, $O_{10} = 10$, $O_{11} = 4$, $O_{12} = 0$, $O_{13} = 1$, and $O_{14} = 1$. Do the observed frequencies conform to Poisson frequencies? (answer: yes, $P(\chi_{10}^2 \geq 12.961) = 0.226$)

---

[15]This study was done in 1898 by the Russian economist and statistician Ladislaus von Bortkiewicz (1868–1931), who first discerned and explained the importance of the Poisson distribution in his book *Das Gesetz der Kleinen Zahlen*. The French mathematician Siméon-Denis Poisson (1781–1840) himself did not recognize the huge practical importance of the distribution that would later be named after him.

Chapter 4

Surprising World of Poisson Probabilities

The Poisson distribution was introduced in section 3.1. This probability distribution is very useful and is as nearly important as the normal probability distribution. In this chapter a number of surprising applications of the Poisson distribution in everyday life are given. The applications include the Santa Claus problem and the coupon collector's problem. These two problems appear in many disguises. You will see that recasting a problem in other ways may be very helpful in solving the problem.

4.1 Fraud in a Canadian lottery

In the Canadian province of Ontario, a strong suspicion arose at a certain point that winning lottery tickets were repeatedly stolen by lottery employees from people who had their lottery ticket checked at a point of sale. These people, mostly the elderly, were then told that their ticket had no prize and that it could go into the trash. The winning ticket was subsequently surrendered by the lottery ticket seller, who pocketed the cash prize. The ball started to roll when an older participant – who always entered the same numbers on his ticket – found out that in 2001 a prize of $250 000 was taken from him by a sales point employee.

How do you prove a widespread fraud in the lottery system? Statistical analysis by Jeffrey Rosenthal, a well-known Canadian professor of probability, showed the fraud. The Poisson distribution played a

79

major role in the analysis. How was the analysis done? Rosenthal worked together with a major Canadian TV channel. Investigation by the TV channel, making an appeal to the freedom of information act, revealed that in the period 1999–2006 there were 5 713 big prizes ($50 000 or more) of which 200 prizes were won by lottery ticket sellers. Can this be explained as a fluke of chance? To answer this question, you need to know how many people are working at the points of sale of the lottery. There were 10 300 sales outlets in Ontario and research by the TV channel led to an estimated average of 3.5 employees per point of sale, or about 36 thousand employees in total. The lottery organization fought this number and came up with 60 thousand lottery ticket sellers. You also need to know how much the average lottery ticket seller spends on the purchase of lottery tickets compared to the average adult inhabitant of Ontario. The estimate of the TV channel was that the average expenditure on lottery tickets taken over all lottery ticket sellers was about 1.5 times as large as the average expenditure on lottery tickets taken over all 8.9 million adult residents of Ontario.

Let's now calculate the probability that the lottery sellers will win 200 or more of the 5 713 big prizes when there are 60 thousand lottery ticket sellers with an expenditure factor of 1.5. In that case the expected number of winners of big prizes among the lottery ticket sellers can be estimated as

$$5\,713 \times \frac{60\,000 \times 1.5}{8\,900\,000} = 57.$$

In view of the physical background of the Poisson distribution – the probability distribution of the total number of successes in a very large number of independent trials each having a very small probability of success – it is plausible to use the Poisson distribution to model the number of winners among the lottery ticket sellers. The Poisson distribution has the nice feature that its standard deviation is the square root of its expected value. Moreover, nearly all the probability mass of the Poisson distribution lies within three standard deviations from the expected value when the expected value is not too small, see section 3.1. Two hundred winners among the lottery ticket sellers lies

$$\frac{200 - 57}{\sqrt{57}} \approx 19$$

standard deviations above the expected value. The probability corresponding to a z-score of 19 is inconceivably small (on the order of 10^{-49}) and makes clear that there is large-scale fraud in the lottery.

The lottery organization objected to the calculations and came with new figures. Does the conclusion of large-scale fraud change for the rosy-tinted figures of 101 000 lottery ticket sellers with an expenditure factor of 1.9? Then you get the estimate

$$5\,713 \times \frac{101\,000 \times 1.9}{8\,900\,000} \approx 123.$$

for the expected number of winners under the lottery ticket sellers. Two hundred winners is still

$$\frac{200 - 123}{\sqrt{123}} \approx 7$$

standard deviations above the expected value. A z-score of 7 has also a negligibly small probability (on the order of 10^{-7}) and cannot be explained as a chance fluctuation. It could not be otherwise that there was large-scale lottery fraud at the sales points of lottery tickets. This suspicion was also supported by other research findings. The investigations led to a great commotion. Headings rolled and the control procedures were adjusted to better protect the customer. The stores' ticket checking machines must now be viewable by customers, and make loud noises to indicate wins. Customers are now required to sign their names on their lottery tickets before redeeming them, to prevent switches.

4.2 Santa Claus and a baby whisperer

In 1996, the James Randi Educational Foundation was founded by James Randi, a former top magician who fought and exposed mockery and pseudo-sciences. The goal of the foundation was to make the public and the media aware of the dangers associated with the performances of psychic mediums. James Randi offered a $1 million prize to anyone who could demonstrate psychic abilities. Obviously, this had to be demonstrated under verifiable test conditions, which would be agreed on beforehand. For example, someone like Uri Geller who claimed to be able to bend spoons without applying force could not bring his own spoons. Different mediums took up the challenge but nobody succeeded. The 'baby whisperer' Derek Ogilvie was one of the mediums who accepted the challenge. This medium claimed to be capable of extrasensory distant observations. He was allowed to choose a child with whom he thought he would have telepathic contact, and he was subjected to the following test. The medium was shown ten different toys that would be given to the child one after the other, in random order, out of sight of the medium. The child was taken to an isolated chamber, and each time the child received a toy, the medium was asked to say what toy it was. If the medium was right six or more times, he would win one million dollars. What is the probability of six or more correct answers?

The problem is in fact a variant of the Santa Claus problem: at a Christmas party, each one of a group of children brings a present, after which the children draw lots randomly to determine who gets which present. What is the probability that none of the children will wind up with their own present? This probability can be easily obtained by the Poisson heuristic. Assume that there are n children at the party and imagine that the children are numbered as $1, 2, \ldots, n$. The Santa Claus problem can be formulated within the framework of a sequence of n trials. In the ith trial, a lot is drawn by the child having number i. Let's say that a trial is successful if the child draws the lot for his/her own present. Then, the success probability of each trial has the same value

$$\frac{(n-1)!}{n!} = \frac{1}{n}$$

(and so the order in which lots are drawn does not matter). Thus the expected value of the number of successes is $n \times \frac{1}{n} = 1$, regardless of the value of n. The outcomes of the trials are not independent of each other, but the dependence is 'weak' if n is sufficiently large. The success probability $\frac{1}{n}$ is small for n large. Then, as noted before in section 3.1, you can use the Poisson heuristic for the probability distribution of the total number of successes. This probability distribution is then approximated by a Poisson distribution with an expected value of 1. Thus, since a 'success' means that the child gets his/her own present, you get for $k = 1, 2, \ldots, n$,

$$P(\text{exactly } k \text{ children will get their own present}) \approx \frac{e^{-1}}{k!}.$$

Numerical investigations reveal that this is a remarkably good approximation for $n \geq 10$ (the first seven decimals of the approximate values agree with the exact values already for n as large as 10). In particular, taking $k = 0$, the probability that none of the children will get their own present is about $\frac{1}{e} = 0.36787\ldots$, or, about 36.8%, regardless of the number of children.

Going back to the ESP experiment with the medium, James Randi was in very little danger of having to cough up the loot. Practically speaking, the probability of six or more correct answers for random guessing is equal to the Poisson probability

$$1 - \sum_{k=0}^{5} \frac{e^{-1}}{k!} = 0.0006,$$

or, about 0.06%. The medium perhaps thought, beforehand, that five correct guesses was the most likely outcome, and a sixth correct guess on top of that wasn't that improbable, so, why not go for it. In the test he had only one correct answer.

4.3 Coupon collector's problem

Suppose that a new brand of breakfast cereal is brought to the market. The producer has introduced a campaign offering a baseball card in each cereal box purchased. There are n different baseball cards. These cards are distributed equally among the cereal boxes so that if a single box is bought there is a $\frac{1}{n}$ chance it will contain a particular baseball card. As a baseball fan, you want to collect a complete set of baseball cards. What are the expected value and the probability mass function of the number of cereal boxes you must buy in order to get all n baseball cards? It is assumed that trading is not an option. The problem is an instance of the so-called *coupon collector's problem*: there are n different types of coupons and each time you obtain a coupon that is equally likely to be any of the n types. How many purchases must be done in order to get a complete collection of coupons? Influencing purchasing behavior by playing on the hoarding impulse of children is an old marketing trick that harkens back to the days when soccer, baseball and celebrity trading cards were the latest thing.

Let's calculate first the expected value of the required number of purchases. Denote by p_i the probability that the next cereal box you purchase will include a card that you haven't yet encountered when you have collected i different cards so far. Then,

$$p_i = \frac{n - i}{n} \quad \text{for } i = 0, 1, \ldots, n - 1.$$

Thus the expected value of the number of cereal boxes you must purchase in order to move from i different cards to $i+1$ different cards is equal to $\frac{n}{n-i}$ for $i = 0, 1, \ldots, n - 1$. This result is intuitively clear by thinking of a repeatable experiment with a success probability of $p = \frac{1}{10}$; then, you would need, on average, $\frac{1}{p} = 10$ trials before achieving a success.[16] Thus, by the linearity property of the expected value, you find that the expected value of the number of purchases necessary for a complete set of cards is:

$$1 + \frac{n}{n - 1} + \frac{n}{n - 2} + \cdots + n = n \left(1 + \frac{1}{2} + \frac{1}{3} + \cdots + \frac{1}{n} \right).$$

An insightful approximation can be given for this expression. In section 1.2 a very accurate approximation is stated for the partial sum of the harmonic series. This leads to the following approximation formula for the expected value of the number of purchases necessary for a complete set of cards:

$$n \left(1 + \frac{1}{2} + \frac{1}{3} + \cdots + \frac{1}{n} \right) \approx n \ln(n) + \gamma n + 0.5,$$

---

[16]Mathematically, the probability that k trials are needed until the first success occurs is $(1 - p)^{k-1}p$ for $k = 1, 2, \ldots$ (the so-called *geometric distribution*). The expected value $\sum_{k=1}^{\infty} k(1-p)^{k-1}p$ is equal to $\frac{p}{p^2} = \frac{1}{p}$, as follows from the formula $\sum_{k=1}^{\infty} kx^{k-1} = \frac{1}{(1-x)^2}$ in section 1.2 with $x = 1-p$. The variance of the geometric distribution can be shown to be $\frac{1-p}{p^2}$.

where $\gamma = 0.57721566\ldots$ is the Euler–Mascheroni constant. This approximation is very accurate already from $n = 10$ onwards. For example, for $n = 10$, the exact expected value is 29.29 and the approximate expected value is 29.30.

The standard deviation of the number of purchases necessary for a complete set of cards is

$$\sqrt{n \sum_{i=0}^{n-1} \frac{i}{(n-i)^2}}.$$

The derivation of this result is based on the fact that the variance of the geometric probability distribution with parameter p is $\frac{1-p}{p^2}$ and the fact that the variance of a finite sum of independent random variables is the sum of the variances of the individual random variables. The details of the derivation are omitted.

What does the probability distribution of the necessary number of purchases look like? The exact distribution demands advanced probability calculations, but a practically useful approximation can be determined fairly easily with the help of the Poisson heuristic. Take a fixed value of r. Then a Poisson approximation to the probability that you would need more than r purchases in order to get a complete collection can be obtained by the following subtle argument. Number the cards as $1, \ldots, n$ and think of the first r purchases as a series of n trials. The ith trial refers to card i and this trial is said be successful if card i is *not* among the first r purchases. The success probability of each trial is

$$\frac{n-1}{n} \times \frac{n-1}{n} \times \cdots \times \frac{n-1}{n} = \left(\frac{n-1}{n}\right)^r.$$

Thus the expected value of the number of successful trials associated with the first r purchases is $n\left(\frac{n-1}{n}\right)^r$. If n is sufficiently large and the success probability $\left(\frac{n-1}{n}\right)^r$ is sufficiently small, the probability distribution of the number of successful trials for the first r purchases can be approximated by a Poisson distribution with expected value $n\left(\frac{n-1}{n}\right)^r$. In particular,

$$P(\text{no success for the first } r \text{ purchases}) \approx e^{-n\left(\frac{n-1}{n}\right)^r}.$$

Table 2: The exact and approximate probabilities

r	100	150	200	250	300	400	500
app	0.9987	0.9106	0.5850	0.2740	0.1101	0.0153	0.0020
exa	0.9998	0.9324	0.6017	0.2785	0.1109	0.0154	0.0020

Translated, the probability of no success is the probability that each of the n cards is among the first r purchases. Therefore, by the complement rule,

$$P(> r \text{ purchases are needed for a complete set}) \approx 1 - e^{-n(\frac{n-1}{n})^r}.$$

For $n = 50$ and several values of r, Table 2 gives the exact and approximate values of the probability that more than r purchases are needed to get a complete collection. You see from the table that the Poisson heuristic gives excellent approximations for practical purposes.

Problem 4.1. The eleven players on a soccer team all have shirts displaying their number. For the upcoming match, each player randomly selects a freshly laundered shirt from the team laundry basket. What is the probability that not a single player will select his own shirt, and what is the probability that more than two players will select their own shirts? (answer: 0.3679 and 0.0803)

Problem 4.2. A blindfolded person is tasting ten different wines. Beforehand, this test subject is informed of the names of the participating wineries, but is not advised as to the order in which the ten wines will be served. The subject may name each winery just once. During the taste-test, the subject succeeds in identifying five of the ten wineries correctly. Do you think this person is a wine connoisseur? (answer: yes, $P(\geq 5$ successes by pure guessing$) = 3.66 \times 10^{-3}$)

Problem 4.3. You are sitting in a class of 15 students. The teacher randomly hands out a graded exam to each student. What is the probability that you will be the only student to get his/her own exam back? (answer: 0.0245)

Problem 4.4. The thirteen cards of a particular suit are taken from a standard deck of 52 playing cards and are thoroughly shuffled. A dealer turns over the cards one at a time, calling out "ace, two, three, ..., king". A match occurs of the card turned over matches the rank called out by the dealer as he turns it over. What is the probability of a match occurring? (answer: $\frac{1}{e} = 0.3679$)

Problem 4.5. The ministate Andorra and its big neighbor Spain have both their own scratch-and-win lottery. In Andorra each of the 10 000 tickets has an open and a covered four-digit number, while in Spain each of the 1 000 000 tickets has an open and a covered seven-digit number. No two tickets contain the same open number or the same covered number, but otherwise the open and covered numbers are randomly distributed over the tickets. If after the scratching of the covered number, it appears that this number is the same as the ticket's open number, then a huge prize is won. Are the probabilities of a win occurring much different in the two lotteries? (answer: no, they are the same)

Problem 4.6. You have a grid of 10 cells in which tokens are placed one by one. Each token is randomly placed into one of the 10 cells. What are the expected value and the standard deviation of the number of tokens necessary until each cell contains at least one token? (answer: 29.29 and 11.21)

Problem 4.7. A fair die is rolled until each of the six possible outcomes has appeared. What are the expected value and the standard deviation of the number of rolls required? (answer: 14.7 and 6.244) What is a Poisson approximation for the probability that more than 12 rolls are needed? (answer: 0.4898)

Problem 4.8. How large should a randomly formed group of people approximately be in order to have a probability of more than 50% that each of 365 possible birthdays (February 29 is excluded) is represented among the people in the group? (answer: 2 285)

Problem 4.9. An airport bus deposits 25 passengers at 7 stops. Each passenger is as likely to get off at any stop as at any other, and the passengers act independently of one another. The bus makes a stop only if someone wants to get off. What is a Poisson approximation to the probability that somebody gets off at each stop? (answer: 0.8621)

Chapter 5

Computer Simulation and Probability

Computer simulation is a natural partner for probability. With simulation, a concrete probability situation can be imitated on the computer. In practice, computer simulation is one of the most used mathematical tools. It is not only a powerful method for getting numerical answers to probability problems, which are otherwise too difficult for an analytical solution, but it is also a very useful tool for adding an extra dimension to the teaching and learning of probability. It may help you gain a better understanding of probabilistic ideas and overcome common misconceptions about the nature of 'randomness'. Simulation may also be helpful for checking answers or for getting quick answers to probability problems.

In the following sections you will see how simulation works and how you can simulate many probability problems with relatively simple tools. You will notice that simulation is not a simple gimmick, but requires mathematical modeling and algorithmic thinking. The emphasis is on the modeling behind computer simulation, not on the programming itself.

5.1 Introduction and random number generators

Suppose you ask somebody to devise a random sequence of H's and T's ('heads' and 'tails') for 100 tosses of a fair coin without having tossed the coin. Most likely you will get a sequence that is far from random. Virtually no one is capable of writing down a sequence of H's and T's that would be statistically indistinguishable from a truly random sequence. Anyone endeavoring to create a random sequence of *H*'s and *T*'s will likely avoid clusters of *H*'s or *T*'s. But such clusters do appear in truly random sequences of heads and tails. Truly random data sets often have unexpected properties that go against intuition. For example, when tossing a fair coin 25 times, the probability of the coin landing on the same side five or more times in a row is about 55%. You may verify this fact by simulating many times the experiment of tossing a fair coin 25 times on the computer. Simulating the experiment of tossing a fair coin 100 times, you will see that the probability of getting a run of either 5 heads or five tails or both is about 97%.

In the simulation of probability models, access to random numbers is of crucial importance. A *random number generator*, as it is called, is indispensable. A random number generator produces random numbers between 0 and 1 (excluding the values 0 and 1). For a 'truly' random number generator, it is as if fate falls on a number between 0 and 1 by pure coincidence. A random number between 0 and 1 is characterized by the property that the probability of the number falling in a subinterval of $(0, 1)$ is the same for each interval of the same length and is equal to the length of the interval. A random number from $(0, 1)$ enables you to simulate, for example, the outcome of a single toss of a fair coin without actually tossing the coin: if the generated random number is between 0 and 0.5 (the probability of this is 0.5), then the outcome of the toss is heads; otherwise, the outcome is tails. In theory, a random number can take on any possible value between 0 and 1. The probability that a truly random number generator will generate a pre-specified number is zero. You can only speak of the probability that the random number will fall in an interval.

Producing random numbers is not as easily accomplished as it seems, especially when they must be generated quickly, efficiently, and in massive amounts. Even for simple simulation experiments the required amount of random numbers runs quickly into the tens of thousands or higher.[17] Generating a very large amount of random

---

[17]In earlier times creative methods were sometimes used to generate random numbers. Around 1 920 crime syndicates in New York City's Harlem used the last

numbers on a one-time only basis, and storing them up in a computer memory, is practically infeasible. But there is a solution to this kind of practical hurdle that is as handsome as it is practical. Instead of generating *truly* random numbers, a computer can generate so-called *pseudo random numbers*, and it achieves this through a nonrandom procedure. This idea comes from the famous Hungarian-American mathematician John von Neumann (1903–1957) who made very important contributions not only to mathematics but also to physics and computer science. The procedure for a pseudo random number generator is iterative by nature and is determined by a suitably chosen function f. Starting with a seed number z_0, numbers $z_1, z_2, \ldots$ are successively generated by

$$z_1 = f(z_0), z_2 = f(z_1), \ldots, z_n = f(z_{n-1}), \ldots .$$

The function f is referred to as a pseudo random number generator and it must be chosen such that the sequence $\{z_i\}$ is statistically indistinguishable from a sequence of truly random numbers. In other words, the output of function f must be able to stand up to a great many statistical tests for 'randomness'. A practically useful feature of a pseudo random number generator is that the sequence $z_1, z_2, \ldots$ of pseudo random numbers is reproducible by using again the same seed z_0. This can come in very handy when you want to make a simulation that compares several designs for a stochastic system: the comparison of alternative designs is purest when it can be achieved under identical experimental conditions.

The older pseudo random number generators are the so-called multiplicative congruential generators. Then the numbers z_n are generated as

$$z_n = az_{n-1} \ (\text{modulo } m),$$

where a and m are appropriately chosen positive integers and the seed number z_0 is a positive integer. The notation $z_n = az_{n-1} \ (\text{modulo } m)$ means that z_n represents the whole remainder of az_{n-1} after division by m; for example, 17 (modulo 5) = 2. This scheme produces one of

---

five digits of the daily published U.S. treasure balance of the American Treasury to generate the winning numbers for their illegal 'Treasury Lottery'.

the numbers $0, 1, \ldots, m-1$ each time. It takes no more than m steps until some number repeats itself. Whenever z_n takes on a value it has had previously, exactly the same sequence of values is generated again, and this cycle repeats itself endlessly. When the parameters a and m are suitably chosen, the number 0 is not generated and each of the numbers $1, \ldots, m-1$ appears exactly once in each cycle. In this case the parameter m gives the length of the cycle. This explains why a very large integer should be chosen for m. The number z_n determines the random number u_n between 0 and 1 by

$$u_n = \frac{z_n}{m}.$$

The quality of the multiplicative congruential generator is strongly dependent on the choice of parameters a and m. A much used generator is characterized as $a = 16\,807$ and $m = 2^{31} - 1$. This generator repeats itself after $m - 1$ values, which is a little over two billion numbers. In the past, this was regarded as plenty. But today, this is not enough for more advanced applications. Nevertheless, the multiplicative congruential generators are still valuable for the simpler applications.

The newest pseudo random number generators do not use the multiplicative congruential scheme. In fact, they do not involve multiplications or divisions at all. These generators are very fast, have incredibly long periods, and provide high-quality pseudo random numbers. In software tools you will find not only the so-called Christopher Columbus generator with a cycle length of about 2^{1492} (at ten million pseudo random numbers per second, it will take more than 10^{434} years before the sequence of numbers will repeat!), but you will also find the Mersenne twister generator with a cycle length of $2^{19937} - 1$. This generator would probably take longer to cycle than the entire future existence of humanity. It has passed numerous tests for randomness, including tests for uniformity of high-dimensional strings of numbers. The modern generators are needed in Monte Carlo simulations requiring huge masses of pseudo random numbers, as is the case in applications in physics and financial engineering.

In the sequel we omit the additive 'pseudo' and simply speak of random numbers and random number generator.

5.2 Simulation tools

Simple tools often suffice for the simulation of probability problems. This section presents several useful tools. These tools include methods to generate a random point inside a bounded region and a random permutation of a finite set of objects.

5.2.1 Simulating a random number from a finite interval

How do you choose randomly a number between two given numbers a and b with $a < b$? To do so, you first use the random number generator to get a random number u between 0 and 1. Next you find a random number x between a and b as

$$x = a + (b - a)u.$$

Verify yourselves that $0 < u < 1$ implies $a < a + (b - a)u < b$.

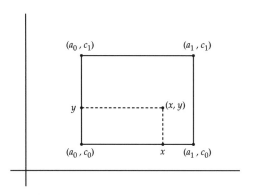

Figure 7: Simulating a random point inside a rectangle

The above procedure can be directly used to generate a random point inside a rectangle. Let (a_0, c_0), (a_1, c_0), (a_0, c_1) and (a_1, c_1) be the four corner points of the rectangle, see Figure 7. You first use the random number generator to get two random numbers u_1 and u_2 from $(0, 1)$. Next you find the random point (x, y) inside the rectangle as

$$x = a_0 + (a_1 - a_0)u_1 \quad \text{and} \quad y = c_0 + (c_1 - c_0)u_2.$$

5.2.2 Simulating a random integer from a finite range

How do you choose randomly an integer from the integers $1, 2, \ldots, M$? To do so, you first use the random number generator to get a random number u between 0 and 1. Next you find a random number k from $1, 2, \ldots, M$ as

$$k = 1 + \text{int}(M \times u).$$

The function $\text{int}(x)$ rounds the number x to the nearest integer that is smaller than or equal to x. That is,

$$\text{int}(x) = k \quad \text{if } k \le x < k + 1$$

for an integer k. As an illustration, suppose you want to simulate the outcome of a single roll of a fair die ($M = 6$). If the random number generator produces $u = 0.60099\ldots$, you get the outcome $1 + \text{int}(6 \times 0.60099\ldots) = 4$. In general, a random integer k from $a, a + 1, \ldots, b$ is obtained as

$$k = a + \text{int}\big((b - a + 1) \times u\big).$$

5.2.3 Simulating a random permutation

Suppose you have 10 people and 10 labels numbered as 1 to 10. How to assign the labels at random such that each person gets assigned a different label? This can be done by making a random permutation of the integers $1, \ldots, 10$ and assigning the labels according to the random order in the permutation. An algorithm for generating a random permutation is useful for many probability problems. A simple and elegant algorithm can be given for generating a random permutation of $(1, 2, \ldots, n)$. The idea of the algorithm is first to randomly choose one of the integers $1, \ldots, n$ and to place that integer in position n. Next you randomly choose one of the remaining $n - 1$ integers and place it in position $n - 1$, etc.

Algorithm for random permutation

1. Initialize $t := n$ and $a[j] := j$ for $j = 1, \ldots, n$.

2. Generate a random number u between 0 and 1.

3. Set $k := 1 + \text{int}(t \times u)$ (random integer from the integers $1, \ldots, t$). Interchange the current values of $a[k]$ and $a[t]$.

4. $t := t - 1$. If $t > 1$, return to step 2; otherwise, stop with the random permutation $(a[1], \ldots, a[n])$.

Numerical example

As an illustration, a random permutation of $(1, 2, 3, 4)$ is constructed.

Iteration 1. $t := 4$. If the generated random number $u = 0.71397\ldots$, then $k = 1 + \text{int}(4 \times 0.71397\ldots) = 3$. Interchanging the elements of the positions $k = 3$ and $t = 4$ in $(1, 2, 3, 4)$ gives $(1, 2, 4, 3)$.
Iteration 2. $t := 3$. If the generated random number $u = 0.10514\ldots$, then $k = 1 + \text{int}(3 \times 0.10514\ldots) = 1$. Interchanging the elements of the positions $k = 1$ and $t = 3$ in $(1, 2, 4, 3)$ gives $(4, 2, 1, 3)$.
Iteration 3. $t := 2$. If the generated random number $u = 0.05982\ldots$, then $k = 1 + \text{int}(2 \times 0.05982\ldots) = 1$. Interchanging the elements of the positions $k = 1$ and $t = 2$ in $(4, 2, 1, 3)$ gives $(2, 4, 1, 3)$.
Iteration 4. $t := 1$. The algorithm stops with the random permutation $(2, 4, 1, 3)$.

Verify yourselves that the algorithm carries literally over to the construction of a random permutation of a finite sequence of objects in which some objects appear multiple times. This is a very useful result.

The algorithm can also be used to simulate a random subset of integers. For example, how to simulate a draw of the lotto $6/45$ in which six distinct numbers are randomly drawn from the number 1 to 45? This can be done by using the algorithm with $n = 45$ and performing only the first 6 iterations until the positions $45, 44, \ldots, 40$ are filled. The elements $a[45], \ldots, a[40]$ in these positions give the six numbers for the lottery draw.

5.2.4 Simulating a random point inside a circle

In section 5.2.1 you have seen how to generate a random point inside a rectangle. How do you generate a random point inside a circle? To do this, you face the complicating factor that the coordinates of a random point inside a circle cannot be generated independently of each other. Any point (x, y) inside a circle with radius r and

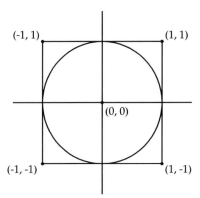

Figure 8: Simulating a random point inside the circle

the origin $(0,0)$ as center must satisfy $x^2 + y^2 < r^2$. A tempting procedure is to generate first a random number $x = a$ from the interval $(-r, r)$ and to generate next a random number y from the interval $(-\sqrt{r^2 - a^2}, \sqrt{r^2 - a^2})$. This procedure, however, violates the requirement that the probability of the random point falling into a subregion should be the same for any two subregions having the same area.

A simple but powerful method to generate a random point inside the circle is the *hit-and-miss method*. The idea of this method is to take a rectangle that envelopes the bounded region and to generate random points inside the rectangle until a point is obtained that falls inside the circle. This simple approach can be used to generate a random point inside any bounded region in the plane. As an illustration, take the unit circle with radius 1 and the origin $(0,0)$ as center. The circle is clamped into the square with the corner points $(-1, -1)$, $(1, -1)$, $(-1, 1)$ and $(1, 1)$, see Figure 8. A random point (x, y) inside this square is found by generating two random numbers u_1 and u_2 from $(0, 1)$ and taking x and y as

$$x = -1 + 2 \times u_1 \quad \text{and} \quad y = -1 + 2 \times u_2.$$

Next you test whether

$$x^2 + y^2 < 1.$$

If this is the case, you have found a random point (x, y) inside the unit circle; otherwise, you repeat the procedure. On average, you have to generate $\frac{4}{\pi} = 1.273$ random points inside the square until you get a random point inside the circle. To see this, note that $\frac{4}{\pi}$ is the ratio of the area of the square and the area of the unit circle.

The idea of the hit-and-miss method is generally applicable. It is often used to find the area of a bounded region in the two-dimensional plane or a higher-dimensional space by enveloping the region by a rectangle or in a higher-dimensional cube. These areas are typically represented by multiple integrals. A classic example of the use of Monte Carlo simulation to compute such integrals goes back to the analysis of neutron diffusion problems in the atomic bomb research at the Los Alamos National Laboratory in 1944. The physicists Nicholas Metropolis and Stanislaw Ulam had to compute multiple integrals representing the volume of a 20-dimensional region and they devised the hit-and-miss method for that purpose.

5.2.5 Simulating from a special probability mass function

Suppose a probability experiment has n possible outcomes $O_1, \ldots, O_n$ with respective probabilities $p_1, \ldots, p_n$. How do you simulate a random outcome? A possible method is the inverse-transformation method. You first generate a random number u between 0 and 1. Then you search for the index l such that $\sum_{k=1}^{l-1} p_k < u \leq \sum_{k=1}^{l} p_k$ and take O_l as random outcome. This method is not practically useful for larger values of n. In the case that each probability p_j is an integer multiple of a fraction $\frac{1}{r}$ for some positive integer r, then there is a very simple method called the *array method*. To explain this method, assume that each probability p_j can be represented by $k_j/100$ for some integer k_j with $0 < k_j < 100$ for $j = 1, \ldots, n$ ($r = 100$). You then form an array A[i], $i = 1, \ldots, 100$, by setting the first k_1 elements equal to O_1, the next k_2 elements equal to O_2, etc., and the last k_n elements equal to O_n. You generate a random number u between 0 and 1 and calculate the random integer $m = 1 + \text{int}(100 \times u)$. Then A[m] is taken as the random outcome of the experiment. As an illustration, suppose that you are asked to determine a substitute result for a canceled football match for which experts believe that the home team would have won with a

Table 3: Simulation results for 100 000 coin tosses

n	$H_n - \frac{1}{2}n$	f_n	n	$H_n - \frac{1}{2}n$	f_n
10	1	0.6000	5 000	−9.0	0.4982
25	1.5	0.5600	7 500	11	0.5015
50	2	0.5400	10 000	24	0.5024
100	2	0.5200	15 000	40	0.5027
250	1	0.5040	20 000	91	0.5045
500	−2	0.4960	25 000	64	0.5026
1 000	10	0.5100	30 000	78	0.5026
2 500	12	0.5048	100 000	129	0.5013

probability of 50%, the visiting team would have won with a probability of 15% and there would have been a draw with a probability of 35%. You can do this by simulating from the probability mass function $(p_1 = 0.50, p_2 = 0.15, p_3 = 0.35)$ on the integers 1, 2 and 3. You form the array A[i], $i = 1, \ldots, 100$ with

$$A[1] = \cdots = A[50] = 1, \ A[51] = \cdots = A[65] = 2,$$
$$A[66] = \cdots = A[100] = 3.$$

You use a random number generator to generate a random number u between 0 and 1. Next you calculate the random integer $k = 1 + \text{int}(100 \times u)$. This is a random integer from $1, \ldots, 100$. Then you take A[m] as the random observation from the probability mass function $(p_1 = 0.50, p_2 = 0.15, p_3 = 0.35)$. For example, suppose that the random number $u = 0.63044 \ldots$ has been generated. This gives $k = 64$. Since $A[64] = 2$, the substitute result for the canceled match is 2 (a win for the visiting team).

5.3 Applications of computer simulation

In this section it is first demonstrated how simulation can be used as a didactic tool to improve one's understanding of randomness. Next you will encounter several probability problems that are analytically difficult to solve, but for which you can quickly and easily find an answer with computer simulation.

5.3.1 Simulation and the law of large numbers

How can you better illustrate the law of large numbers than with the simulation study in which a coin is repeatedly tossed? Such a simulation experiment may improve your intuition about randomness. The law of large numbers says that the percentage of coin tosses to come out heads will be as close to 50% as you can imagine, provided that the number of coin tosses is large enough. But how large is large enough? Table 3 presents several intermediate results of a simulation study in which a fair coin is tossed 100 000 times. As said before, the simulation of the outcome of a single coin toss requires only one random number u from $(0, 1)$: if $u \leq 0.5$, the outcome is heads; otherwise, it is tails. In the table, the statistic $H_n - \frac{1}{2}n$ gives the simulated number of heads minus the expected number after n tosses, and the statistic f_n gives the simulated relative frequency of heads after n tosses. It is worthwhile to take a close look at the results in the table. You see that the realization of the relative frequency, f_n, indeed approaches the true value 0.5 of the probability of heads in a rather irregular manner and converges more slowly than most of us would expect intuitively. You should be suspicious of the outcomes of simulation studies that consist of only a small number of simulation runs, see also section 5.4. This is particularly true for simulations that deal with very small probabilities!

5.3.2 Geometric probability problems

Geometric probability problems constitute a class of probability problems that often seem very simple but are sometimes very difficult to solve analytically. Take the problem of finding the expected value of the distance between two random points inside the unit square (sides with length 1) and the expected value for two random points inside the unit circle (radius 1). The analytical derivation of these expected values requires advanced integral calculus and leads to the following exact results:

$$\frac{1}{15} \left[2 + \sqrt{2} + 5 \ln(1 + \sqrt{2}) \right] \approx 0.5214 \quad \text{and} \quad \frac{128}{45\pi} \approx 0.9054.$$

It is a piece of cake to estimate the expected values by computer simulation. How does the simulation program look like? Perform a very large number of simulation runs. In each simulation run two random points (x_1, y_1) and (x_2, y_2) are generated, using the method in subsection 5.2.1 for the unit square and using the method in subsection 5.2.3 for the unit circle. In each run the distance between the two points is calculated by Pythagoras as

$$\sqrt{(x_1 - x_2)^2 + (y_1 - y_2)^2}.$$

Then, the average of the distances found in the simulation runs is calculated. By the law of large numbers, the average gives an estimate for the expected value of the distance between two random points. Many simulation runs are needed to get accurate estimates. The question of how many runs should be done will be addressed in the next section. In one million simulation runs the estimates 0.521 and 0.906 were obtained for the expected values of the distances between two random point inside the unit square and between two random points inside the unit circle. Also, an estimate for the standard deviation of the distance between two random points can be directly obtained with simulation. The estimates 0.247 and 0.424 were found for the unit square and the unit circle. For the interested reader Python computer programs are given in an appendix to this chapter. The computing times for the one million simulation runs are a matter of seconds on a fast computer.

5.3.3 Birthday problems

In the classic birthday problem the question is what the probability is that two or more people share a birthday in a randomly formed group of people. This problem has been analytically solved in section 1.2. It was easy to find the answer. The problem becomes much more difficult when the question is what the probability is that two or more people have a birthday within one day from each other. This is the *almost-birthday problem*. However, the simulation program for the almost-birthday problem is just as simple as the simulation program for the birthday problem. An outline of the simulation programs is as follows. The starting point is a randomly formed group of m people (no twins), where each day is equally likely as birthday for any person. For ease, it is assumed that the year has 365 days (February 29 is excluded). For each of the two birthday problems, a very large number of simulation runs is performed. In each simulation run, m random integers $g_1, \ldots, g_m$ are generated, where the random integer g_i represents the birthday of the ith person. Each of these integers is randomly chosen from the integers $1, \ldots, 365$, using the simulation tool in section 5.2.2. In each simulation run for the classic birthday problem you test whether there are distinct indices i and j such that

$$|g_i - g_j| = 0,$$

while in each simulation run for the almost-birthday problem you test whether there are distinct indices i and j such that

$$|g_i - g_j| \leq 1 \text{ or } |g_i - g_j| = 364.$$

You find an estimate for the sought probability by dividing the number of simulation runs for which the test criterion is satisfied by the total number of runs. As you see, the simulation program for the almost-birthday problem is just as simple as that for the classic birthday problem.

5.3.4 Lottery problem

What is the probability of getting two or more consecutive numbers when six distinct numbers are randomly drawn from the numbers 1 to 45 in the lotto 6/45? The exact formula $1 - \binom{40}{6}/\binom{45}{6}$ can be given for this probability, but the argument to get this formula is far from simple. However this probability, which is surprisingly large, can be quickly and easily obtained by computer simulation. In each simulation run you get the six lottery numbers by applying six iterations of the algorithm in section 5.2.3 and taking the six integers in the array elements $a[45], a[44], \ldots, a[40]$. Next you test whether there are consecutive numbers among these six numbers. This is easily done by checking whether $a[i] - a[j]$ is 1 or -1 for some i and j with $40 \leq i, j \leq 45$. The probability of drawing two consecutive numbers is estimated by dividing the number of simulations runs for which the test criterion is satisfied by the total number of simulation runs. One million simulation runs resulted in the estimate 0.5289. The simulation program needs only a minor modification to simulate the probability of getting three consecutive numbers. Simulation leads to the estimate 0.056 for this probability. An analytical solution seems not possible.

5.3.5 The Mississippi problem

An amusing but very difficult combinatorial probability problem is the Mississippi problem. What is the probability that any two adjacent letters are different in a random permutation of the eleven letters of the word Mississippi? A simulation model can be constructed by identifying the letter m with the number 1, the letter i with the number 2, the letter s with the number 3, and the letter p with the number 4. In each simulation run a random permutation of the sequence $(1, 2, 3, 3, 2, 3, 3, 2, 4, 4, 2)$ is constructed by using an obvious modification of the permutation algorithm in section 5.2.3: the initialization of the algorithm now becomes $a[1] = 1$, $a[2] = 2$, ..., $a[10] = 4$, $a[11] = 2$. To test whether any two adjacent numbers are different in the resulting random permutation $(a[1], a[2], \ldots, a[11])$, you check whether $a[i + 1] - a[i] \neq 0$ for $i = 1, \ldots, 10$. The estimate 0.058 was obtained for the sought probability after 100 000 simulation runs.

It is never possible to achieve perfect accuracy through simulation. All you can measure is how likely the estimate is to be correct. This issue will be discussed in the next section. You will see that, if you want to achieve one more decimal digit of precision in the estimate, you have to increase the number of simulation runs with a factor of about one hundred. In other words, the probabilistic error bound decreases as the reciprocal square root of the number of simulation runs. The square root law is here at work.

5.4 Statistical analysis of simulation output

How many simulation runs should be made in order to get a desired level of accuracy in the estimate? When doing a simulation, it is important to have a probabilistic judgment about the accuracy of the point estimate. Such a judgment is provided by the concept of confidence interval. Suppose that you want to estimate the unknown probability p of a particular event E. If n simulation runs are performed and the event E occurs in s of these n runs, then

$$\hat{p} = \frac{s}{n}$$

is the estimate for the true value of the probability p. The accuracy of this estimate is expressed by the 95% confidence interval

$$\left(\hat{p} - 1.96\frac{\sqrt{\hat{p}(1 - \hat{p})}}{\sqrt{n}}, \ \hat{p} + 1.96\frac{\sqrt{\hat{p}(1 - \hat{p})}}{\sqrt{n}}\right).$$

The confidence interval can be obtained from an application of the central limit theorem to the binomial distribution. The details of the derivation are not given. The 95% confidence interval should be interpreted as follows: with a probability of about 95% the interval will cover the true value of p if n is large enough. In other words, if you construct a large number of 95% confidence intervals, each based on the same number of simulation runs, then the proportion of intervals covering the true value of p is about 0.95.

The effect of n on the term $\sqrt{\hat{p}(1 - \hat{p})}$ fades away quickly if n gets larger. This means that the width of the confidence interval is nearly proportional to $1/\sqrt{n}$ for n sufficiently large. This conclusion leads to a practically important rule of thumb:

to reduce the width of a confidence interval by a factor of two, about four times as many observations are needed.

This is a very useful rule for simulation purposes. Let's illustrate this with the almost-birthday problem with a group of 20 people. For the probability that two or more people will have their birthdays within one day of each other, a simulation with 25 000 runs results in the probability estimate of 0.8003 with (0.7953, 0.8052) as 95% confidence interval, whereas 100 000 simulation runs result in an estimate of 0.8054 with (0.8029, 0.8078) as 95% confidence interval. The confidence interval has indeed been narrowed by a factor of two. The interval was reduced to (0.8028, 0.8053) after 400 000 runs.

How can you construct a confidence interval if the simulation study is set up to estimate an unknown expected value of some random variable X rather than an unknown probability? Letting $X_1, \ldots, X_n$ represent the observations for X resulting from n simulation runs, the expected value $\mu = E(X)$ and the standard deviation $\sigma = \sigma(X)$

are estimated by

$$\hat{\mu} = \frac{1}{n}\sum_{k=1}^{n} X_k \quad \text{and} \quad \hat{\sigma} = \sqrt{\frac{1}{n}\sum_{k=1}^{n} X_k^2 - \hat{\mu}^2}.$$

Then, the corresponding 95% confidence interval for the estimate $\hat{\mu}$ is

$$\left(\hat{\mu} - 1.96\frac{\hat{\sigma}}{\sqrt{n}},\ \hat{\mu} + 1.96\frac{\hat{\sigma}}{\sqrt{n}}\right).$$

Simulation modeling problems

In each of the following modeling problems you are asked to set up a mathematical model for a simulation program for the problem in question. Computer programming is beyond the scope of this book. However, if you master a programming language, it may be fun to write a simulation program for some of the problems.

Problem 5.1. Set up a simulation model in order to estimate the probability that the equation $Ax^2 + Bx + C = 0$ has two real roots if A, B and C are randomly chosen integers from $1, 2, \ldots, 100$.

Problem 5.2. You pick repeatedly a random number from $1, 2, \ldots$, 100 until the sum of the picked integers is more than 100. Set up a simulation model in order to estimate the expected value and the standard deviation of the number of picks needed.

Problem 5.3. You pick repeatedly a random number from $(0, 1)$ and add these numbers until the sum is larger than 1. Set up a simulation model in order to estimate the expected value and the standard deviation of the number of picks needed.

Problem 5.4. A stick is broken at two places. The break points are chosen at random on the stick, independently of each other. Set up a simulation model to estimate the probability that a triangle can be formed with the three pieces of the broken stick. *Hint*: a triangle can be formed from three line segments with lengths a, b and c if and only if $a > b + c$, $b > a + c$ and $c > a + b$.

Problem 5.5. Set up a simulation model in order to estimate the expected value and the standard deviation of the area of the triangle that is formed by three randomly chosen points inside the unit square. Do the same for three randomly chosen points inside the unit circle. *Hint*: the area of a triangle with sides of lengths a, b and c is $\sqrt{s(s-a)(s-b)(s-c)}$, where $s = \frac{1}{2}(a+b+c)$.

Problem 5.6. Let $f(x)$ be a positive function on a finite interval (a, b) such that $0 \leq f(x) \leq M$ for $a \leq x \leq b$. How can you use simulation to estimate the integral $\int_a^b f(x)\,dx$?

Problem 5.7. Set up a simulation model in order to estimate the expected value and standard deviation of the distance between two randomly chosen points inside the unit cube. Do the same for the unit sphere.

Problem 5.8. You randomly choose two points inside a circle. Set up a simulation model in order to estimate the probability that these two random points and the center of the circle form an obtuse triangle (an obtuse triangle is one with an angle greater than 90°). Do the same for a sphere in which two random points are chosen.

Problem 5.9. Seven students live in a student house. Set up a simulation model to estimate the probability that two or more of these students have their birthdays within one week of each other.

Problem 5.10. Three British teams are among the eight teams that have reached the quarter-finals of the Champions League soccer. Set up a simulation model in order to estimate the probability that the three British teams will avoid each other in the draw if the eight teams are paired randomly.

Problem 5.11. The eight teams that have reached the quarter-finals of the Champions League soccer consist of two British teams, two German teams, two Italian teams and two Spanish teams. Set up a simulation model in order to estimate the probability that no two teams from the same country will be paired in the quarter-finals draw if the eight teams are paired randomly.

Problem 5.12. Using a standard deck of 52 playing cards, you pick two different card ranks (say, an ace and a seven). Then the cards are thoroughly shuffled and are dealt out face-up in a straight line. Set up a simulation model in order to estimate the probability that you will find your chosen two ranks as neighbors (the suit of a card is not relevant).

Problem 5.13. A standard deck of 52 playing cards is thoroughly shuffled after which the cards are turned over one by one. Set up a simulation model in order to estimate the probability of getting either 5 red cards or 5 black cards or both in a row.

Problem 5.14. A fair die is rolled until the run 123456 appears. Set up a simulation model in order to estimate the probability that such a run will appear within 500 rolls.

Problem 5.15. In order to introduce a new kind of chips, the producer has introduced a campaign offering a flippo in each bag of chips purchased. There are five different flippos $F_1, \ldots, F_5$. Each bag contains one flippo and this is flippo F_i with probability p_i, where $p_1 = 0.05$, $p_2 = 0.20$, $p_3 = 0.20$, $p_4 = 0.25$ and $p_5 = 0.30$. Set up a simulation model in order to estimate the expected value and the standard deviation of the number of purchases needed for a complete collection of flippos.

Problem 5.16. You repeatedly roll two fair dice until each of the 11 possible values of the sum of a single roll with two dice has appeared. Set up a simulation model in order to estimate the expected value and the standard deviation of the number of rolls needed.

Problem 5.17. You play the following game. A fair die is rolled until a 1, 3, 5, or 6 appears. If the game ends with a 6, you get paid out in dollars the number of times the die has been rolled; otherwise, you get nothing paid out. Set up a simulation model in order to estimate the expected value and the standard deviation of the amount you get paid out.

Problem 5.18. You play the following game. A fair coin will be tossed 10 times. At each toss you have to decide how much of your bankroll to stake. If the outcome of the toss is heads, you get back twice your stake; otherwise, you get back a quarter of your stake. Starting with a bankroll of $100, your strategy is to stake half your bankroll each time. Set up a simulation model in order to estimate the expected value and the standard deviation of your end capital and the probability of ending up with a bankroll of no more than $(\frac{15}{16})^5 \times 100$ dollars.

Problem 5.19. A carnival booth offers the following game of chance. Under each of six inverted cups is a colored ball, in some random order. The six balls are colored red, blue, yellow, orange, green and purple. You wager $5 to play and you get six tokens. All you have to do is to guess the color of the ball under each of the cups, where you must handle one cup at a time. Every time you guess, you risk a token. If your guess is wrong, you lose the token. Each time you guess correctly, the ball is uncovered and you keep your token. If you can guess all six balls before you run out of tokens, you are paid out $20; otherwise, you lose your stake of $5. Set up a simulation model in order to estimate the average amount won by the carnival booth owner per game in the long-run.

Problem 5.20. An opaque bowl contains 11 envelopes in the colors of red and blue. You are told that there are four envelopes of one color each containing $100 and seven empty envelopes of the other color, but you cannot see the envelopes in the bowl. The envelopes are taken out of the bowl, one by one and in random order. Each time an envelope has been taken out, you must decide whether or not to open this envelope. Once you have opened an envelope, you get the money in that envelope (if any) and the process stops. Your stopping rule is to open the envelope drawn as soon as four or more envelopes of each color have been taken out of the bowl. Set up a simulation model in order to estimate the probability of winning $100.

Appendix: Python programs for simulation

The two Python programs in this appendix are meant to give the reader not having programming experience some idea of how a computer program for simulation works. Python is a relatively simple programming language and is easy to learn since it requires a unique syntax that focuses on readability. The text after # is comment, which is not read by the program but is meant as explanation for the reader.

Python code for the distance between two random points inside unit square

```
import numpy as np # package for numerical computations
import numpy.random as rnd # package for random numbers
import numpy.linalg as la # package for linear algebra computations

def randompointinunitsquare():
    # returns a random point in the unit square
    return rnd.rand(2)

def simulation(n): # this function generates n pairs of points (P, Q)
    delta = np.zeros(n) # allocates an array of length n
    for i in range(n): # n pairs of points
        P = randompointinunitsquare()
        Q = randompointinunitsquare()
        delta[i] = la.norm(P − Q) # distance between P and Q
    return delta

def main(): # the parameters are set and the output is printed
    n = 1000000 # number of simulation runs
    rnd.seed(15534) # seed 15534 starts random number generator
    delta = simulation(n) # output of the simulation() function
    print('average :', np.mean(delta)) # expected value of distance
    print('variance:', np.var(delta)) # variance of distance

main()
```

Python code for the distance between two random points inside unit circle

```
import numpy as np # package for numerical computations
import numpy.random as rnd # package for random numbers
import numpy.linalg as la # package for linear algebra computations

def randompointinunitcirle(): # returns a random point P in unit circle
    hit = 0
    while hit==0: # hit-and-miss method
        P = -1 + 2× rnd.rand(2) # random point in square
        hit = la.norm(P)< 1 # accept P if P in circle, otherwise repeat
    return P

def simulation(n): # this function generates n pairs of points (P, Q)
    delta = np.zeros(n) # allocates an array of length n
    for i in range(n): # n pairs of points
        P = randompointinunitcirle()
        Q = randompointinunitcirle()
        delta[i] = la.norm(P − Q) # distance between P and Q
    return delta

def main(): # the parameters are set and the output is printed
    n = 1000000 # number of simulation runs
    rnd.seed(15534) # seed 15534 starts random number generator
    delta = simulation(n) # output of the simulation() function
    print('average :', np.mean(delta)) # expected value of distance
    print('variance:', np.var(delta)) # variance of distance

main()
```

Solutions to Selected Problems

Fully worked-out solutions to a number of problems are given. Including worked-out solutions is helpful for students who use the book for self-study and stimulates active learning. Make sure you try the problems before looking at the solutions.

2.3. Two methods will be presented to solve this problem. It is always helpful if you can check the solution using alternative solution methods.

Solution method 1: This method uses an ordered sample space. Imagining that the eight heads of states are labeled as $h_1, h_2, \ldots, h_8$, the sample space consists all possible orderings of $h_1, h_2, \ldots, h_8$. Each of the 8! possible orderings is equally likely. If the positions of the presidents of China and the U.S. are fixed, there remain 6! possible orderings for the other six statesmen. The presidents of China and the U.S. stand next to each other if they take up the positions i and $i + 1$ for some i with $1 \leq i \leq 7$. In the case that these two statesmen take up the positions i and $i+1$, there are 2! possibilities for the order among them. Thus, there are $6! \times 7 \times 2!$ orderings in which the presidents of China and the U.S. stand next to each other, and so

$$P(\text{the two presidents will stand next to each other}) = \frac{6! \times 7 \times 2!}{8!} = \frac{1}{4}.$$

Solution method 2: This method uses an unordered sample space. The sample space consists of all possible combinations of the two positions for the presidents of China and the U.S. with order not mattering. This sample space has $\binom{8}{2} = 28$ equally likely elements. The number of elements for which the two presidents stand next to each other is 7. Thus the probability that they stand next to each other is $\frac{7}{28} = \frac{1}{4}$.

2.7. If the sets A and B are not disjoint, then $P(A) + P(B)$ counts twice the probability of the set of outcomes that belong to both A and B. Therefore $P(A \text{ and } B)$ should be subtracted from $P(A) + P(B)$.

2.9. Translate the problem into choosing a point at random inside the unit square. The probability that the two persons will meet within 10 minutes of each other is equal to the probability that a point chosen at random in the unit square will fall inside the shaded region, see the figure. The area of the shaded region is calculated as $1 - \frac{5}{6} \times \frac{5}{6} = \frac{11}{36}$. Dividing this by the area of the unit square, you get that the desired probability is $\frac{11}{36}$.

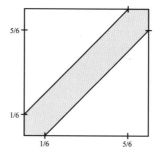

2.12. Imagine that the two cards are picked one by one. Then, using the product rule, the probability of getting two red cards is $\frac{14}{21} \times \frac{13}{20} = \frac{13}{30}$ and the probability of getting one red card and one black card is $\frac{14}{21} \times \frac{7}{20} + \frac{7}{21} \times \frac{14}{20} = \frac{14}{30}$. Alternatively, the solution can be obtained by using the urn model from section 1.1: the probability of getting two red cards is $\binom{14}{2}/\binom{21}{2} = \frac{13}{30}$ and the probability of getting one red card and one black card is $\binom{14}{1}\binom{7}{1}/\binom{21}{2} = \frac{14}{30}$.

2.20. Let A be the event that there is originally a piranha in the bowl and B be the event that the removed fish is a piranha. The sought-after probability is $P(A \mid B)$. This probability can be calculated as

$$P(A \mid B) = \frac{P(A \text{ and } B)}{P(B)} = \frac{P(A)P(B \mid A)}{P(B)}.$$

The probability $P(A) = \frac{1}{2}$ and the probability $P(B \mid A) = 1$. Denoting by $\overline{A}$ the event that the original fish in the bowl is not a piranha and using the law of conditional probability, you get

$$P(B) = P(B \mid A)P(A) + P(B \mid \overline{A})P(\overline{A}) = 1 \times \frac{1}{2} + \frac{1}{2} \times \frac{1}{2} = \frac{3}{4}.$$

Therefore the sought-after probability is given by $P(A \mid B) = \frac{1/2}{3/4} = \frac{2}{3}$. An alternative way to get this answer is to use Bayes' rule in odds form from section 2.4.

2.21. Let A be the event that you ever win the jackpot by buying a ticket only once. The event A can only occur if one of the disjoint events B_1 and B_2 occurs, where B_1 is the event of having six correctly predicted numbers on your first ticket and B_2 is the event of having exactly two correctly predicted numbers on your first ticket. Then, $P(A) = P(A \mid B_1)P(B_1) + P(A \mid B_2)P(B_2)$. Using the urn model from section 1.1, $P(B_1) = 1/\binom{45}{6}$ and $P(B_2) = \binom{6}{2}\binom{39}{4}/\binom{45}{6}$. Also, $P(A \mid B_1) = 1$ and $P(A \mid B_2) = P(A)$. This leads to the equation

$$P(A) = 1 \times \frac{1}{\binom{45}{6}} + P(A) \times \frac{\binom{6}{2}\binom{39}{4}}{\binom{45}{6}},$$

which gives $P(A) = 1.447 \times 10^{-7}$.

2.25. Let the hypothesis H be the event that the inhabitant you overheard spoke truthfully and the evidence E be the event that the other inhabitant says that the inhabitant you overheard spoke the truth. The prior distribution is $P(H) = \frac{1}{3}$ and $P(\overline{H}) = \frac{2}{3}$. Also, the likelihood ratio has $P(E \mid H) = \frac{1}{3}$ and $P(E \mid \overline{H}) = \frac{2}{3}$. Thus the posterior odds of hypothesis H are

$$\frac{P(H \mid E)}{P(\overline{H} \mid E)} = \frac{1/3}{2/3} \times \frac{1/3}{2/3} = \frac{1}{4},$$

and so the posterior probability of hypothesis H is $\frac{1/4}{1+1/4} = \frac{1}{5}$.

2.27. Let the hypothesis H be the event that the standard die was picked and let the evidence E_1 be the event that the first roll of the picked die has the outcome 6. The prior probabilities are $P(H) = P(\overline{H}) = \frac{1}{2}$ and the likelihood ratio has $P(E_1 \mid H) = \frac{1}{6}$ and $P(E_1 \mid \overline{H}) = \frac{1}{3}$. Thus the posterior odds of the hypothesis H are

$$\frac{P(H \mid E_1)}{P(\overline{H} \mid E_1)} = \frac{1/2}{1/2} \times \frac{1/6}{1/3} = \frac{1}{2},$$

which gives the updated value $\frac{1/2}{1+1/2} = \frac{1}{3}$ for the probability that the standard die was picked. The second question can be answered in two ways. After the first roll has been done but before the second roll will be done, you take the posterior probabilities $P(H \mid E) = \frac{1}{3}$ and $P(\overline{H} \mid E) = \frac{2}{3}$ as the prior probabilities for $P(H)$ and $P(\overline{H})$. Doing so and letting E_2 be the event that the second roll has the outcome 6, you get

$$\frac{P(H \mid E_2)}{P(\overline{H} \mid E_2)} = \frac{1/3}{2/3} \times \frac{1/6}{1/3} = \frac{1}{4},$$

and so the newly updated value of the probability that the standard die was picked is $\frac{1}{5}$. Alternatively, this probability can be calculated by letting the evidence $E_{1,2}$ be the event that each of the first two rolls of the picked die has outcome 6. Then, before the first two rolls are done, the prior probabilities $P(H)$ and $P(\overline{H})$ are each equal to $\frac{1}{2}$ and the likelihood ratio has $P(E_{1,2} \mid H) = \frac{1}{6} \times \frac{1}{6}$ and $P(E_{1,2} \mid \overline{H}) = \frac{1}{3} \times \frac{1}{3}$. This leads to

$$\frac{P(H \mid E_{1,2})}{P(\overline{H} \mid E_{1,2})} = \frac{1/2}{1/2} \times \frac{1/36}{1/9} = \frac{1}{4},$$

which gives again the update $\frac{1}{5}$ for the probability that the standard die was picked. The Bayesian approach has the feature that you can continuously update your beliefs as information accrues. Verify yourselves that the updated value of the probability that the standard die was picked becomes $\frac{1}{9}$ after a third roll with outcome 2. *Note:* this problem nicely illustrates the Bayesian view that probabilities represent the knowledge an observer has about the state of nature of a physical object.

2.30. The possible values of the random variable X are 20 cents, 35 cents, and 50 cents. Imagine that the two coins are picked one by one. Then, using the product rule for conditional probabilities, $P(X = 20) =$

$\frac{3}{5} \times \frac{2}{4} = \frac{3}{10}$, $P(X = 35) = \frac{3}{5} \times \frac{2}{4} + \frac{2}{5} \times \frac{3}{4} = \frac{6}{10}$, and $P(X = 50) = \frac{2}{5} \times \frac{1}{4} = \frac{1}{10}$. *Note:* The underlying sample space of X has not been specified. This is often not done when calculating the probability distribution of a random variable. The sample space $\{(D, D), (D, Q), (Q, D), (Q, Q)\}$ could have been chosen, where the outcome (D, D) occurs if the first coin taken is a dime and the second one is also a dime, the outcome (D, Q) occurs if the first coin taken is a dime and the second one is a quarter, etc.

2.33. By the linearity property of the expected value,

$$E[(aX + b)^2] = E[a^2X^2 + 2abX + b^2] = a^2E(X^2) + 2abE(X) + b^2.$$

Also, $\left(E(aX + b)\right)^2 = \left(aE(X) + b\right)^2 = a^2\left(E(X)\right)^2 + 2abE(X) + b^2$. Thus $\sigma^2(aX + b)$ is equal to

$$E[(aX + b)^2] - \left(E(aX + b)\right)^2 = a^2E(X^2) - a^2\left(E(X)\right)^2$$
$$= a^2\sigma^2(X).$$

2.34. By the definitions of expected value and variance, $E(X) = 0 \times (1-p) + 1 \times p = p$ and $\sigma^2(X) = (0-p)^2 \times (1-p) + (1-p)^2 \times p = p(1-p)$ and so $\sigma(X) = \sqrt{p(1 - p)}$.

3.4. The probability of getting 26 or more sixes in 13 rolls of 10 dice is the same as the probability of getting 26 or more sixes in 130 rolls of a single die. Using the binomial distribution with parameters $n = 130$ and $p = \frac{1}{6}$, the desired probability is equal to

$$\sum_{k=26}^{130} \binom{130}{k} \left(\frac{1}{6}\right)^k \left(\frac{5}{6}\right)^{130-k} = 0.1820.$$

Let the random variable X be your payout per dollar staked in the game. The random variable X takes on the values 0 and 5 with respective probabilities 0.1820 and 0.8180. Thus $E(X) = 0 \times 0.8180 + 5 \times 0.1820 = 0.91$ dollar. Since $E(X) < 1$, the game is unfavorable to you. The house percentage is 9%.

3.8. An appropriate model is the Poisson model. The sought probability can be estimated as $e^{-20/400} \approx 0.951$.

3.11. Let the $N(\mu, \sigma^2)$ distributed random variable X be the length of a gestation period, where $\mu = 280$ days and $\sigma = 10$ days. Using the basic result that $\frac{X-\mu}{\sigma}$ is $N(0, 1)$ distributed if X is $N(\mu, \sigma^2)$ distributed, the probability that a birth is more than 15 days overdue is equal to

$$P(X > 295) = P\left(\frac{X - 280}{10} > \frac{295 - 280}{10}\right)$$

$$= 1 - P\left(\frac{X - 280}{15} \le \frac{295 - 280}{10}\right) = 1 - \Phi(1.5) = 0.0668.$$

In other words, the proportion of births that are more than 15 days overdue is 6.68%.

3.15. Let X denote the demand for the item. The normally distributed random variable X has an expected value of $\mu = 100$ and satisfies $P(X > 125) = 0.05$. To find the standard deviation σ of X, write $P(X > 125) = 0.05$ as

$$P\left(\frac{X - 100}{\sigma} > \frac{125 - 100}{\sigma}\right) = 1 - \Phi\left(\frac{25}{\sigma}\right) = 0.05.$$

Thus $\Phi\left(\frac{25}{\sigma}\right) = 0.95$. The percentile $\xi_{0.95} = 1.645$ is the unique solution to the equation $\Phi(x) = 0.95$. Thus $\frac{25}{\sigma} = 1.645$, which gives $\sigma = 15.2$.

3.18. Suppose that the game is played n times with a stake of one dollar in each game. The net profit of the casino in the ith game is $W_i = 1 - 2X_i$, where the Bernoulli variable X_i is 0 with probability $\frac{19}{37}$ and is 1 with probability $\frac{18}{37}$. Since $E(X_i) = \frac{18}{37}$ and $\sigma(X_i) = \sqrt{(18/37) \times (19/37)}$, the expected value and the standard deviation of W_i are equal to $\mu = \frac{1}{37}$ and $\sigma = 2 \times \sqrt{(18/37) \times (19/37)}$. The net profit of the casino after n games is distributed as $W_1 + \cdots + W_n$ and has approximately a normal distribution with expected value $n\mu$ and standard deviation $\sigma\sqrt{n}$ for n large. It is interesting to have a look at the probability that the net profit of the casino after n games will be negative. This probability is given by $P(W_1 + \cdots + W_n \le 0)$ and can be evaluated as

$$P\left(\frac{W_1 + \cdots + W_n - n\mu}{\sigma\sqrt{n}} \le \frac{-n\mu}{\sigma\sqrt{n}}\right) \approx \Phi\left(\frac{-n\mu}{\sigma\sqrt{n}}\right) = \Phi\left(\frac{-\sqrt{n}}{2\sqrt{18 \times 19}}\right).$$

The probability has the values 0.0034, 9.6×10^{-6} and 7.4×10^{-10} for $n = 10\,000$, $25\,000$ and $50\,000$. These results clearly illustrate that the probability is practically equal to zero that the casino will lose over the long run. There is a steadily growing riskless profit for the casino! Suppose that n games with one dollar stakes are to be played. Then there is an about 99% probability that the net profit of the casino after the n bets will be larger than $\frac{n}{37} - 2.236\sqrt{n}$ for n large, as you may verify by solving x from $P(W_1 + \cdots + W_n > x) = 0.99$.

3.21. By the memoryless property of the exponential distribution, the number of births between twelve o'clock midnight and six o'clock in the morning is independent of what happened before twelve o'clock midnight. Since the births occur according to a Poisson process with a rate of $\lambda = \frac{5}{24}$ births per hour, the number of births between twelve o'clock midnight and six o'clock in the morning has a Poisson distribution with an expected value of $\lambda \times 6 = \frac{5}{4}$. The probability that this number of births is larger than two is equal to $1 - e^{-5/4} \frac{(5/4)^k}{k!} = 0.1315$.

4.3. If you get back your own exam and none of the other 14 students gets back their own exams, then you are the only person who gets back the own exam. Let A be the event that you get back your own exam and B be the event that none of the other 14 students gets back their own exams. Then, the desired probability is $P(A \text{ and } B)$. The product rule gives $P(A \text{ and } B) = P(A)P(A \mid B)$. The probability $P(A)$ is $\frac{1}{15}$, while the conditional probability $P(A \mid B)$ is nothing else than the probability that no child picks his/her own present in the Santa Claus problem with 14 children. Thus $P(A \mid B) = e^{-1}$, and so the probability that you are the only person who gets back the own exam is $\frac{e^{-1}}{15} = 0.0245$.

4.9. This problem can be translated into the coupon collector's problem with $n = 7$ coupons. The probability that the bus with 25 passengers makes a stop at each of the 7 stops is nothing else than the probability that no more than $r = 25$ coupons are needed in order to collect all coupons. Therefore the probability that the bus will make 7 stops is approximately equal to the Poisson probability $e^{-7 \times (6/7)^{25}} = 0.8621$. This is an excellent approximation (the exact value can be shown to be 0.8562).

5.12. It is no restriction to assume that the ranks ace and seven have been chosen. The idea is to give the four aces the label 1, the four sevens the label 2, and each of the other 44 cards the label 4. In each simulation run you generate a random permutation of the sequence $(1, 1, 1, 1, 2, 2, 2, 2, 4, \ldots, 4)$. Next you test whether the random permutation $(a[1], a[2], \ldots, a[52])$ satisfies $a[i + 1] - a[i]$ is 1 or -1 for some i. The desired probability is estimated by dividing the number of simulation runs for which the test criterion is satisfied by the total number of simulation runs.

5.14. As is often the case, several simulation approaches are possible. In a straightforward simulation approach, each simulation run consists of generating 500 random integers from 1 to 6 and forming an array $(O[1], \ldots, O[500])$, where $O[i]$ contains the ith generated integer. Next you test whether there is an index i such that $O[i] = 1$, $O[i + 1] = 2$, $\ldots$, $O[i + 5] = 6$. In a more subtle simulation approach, you use a state variable having the value 0 for the starting state, the value 1 if the outcome of the last roll is 1, the value 2 if the outcome of the last two rolls is 12, etc., and the value 6 if the outcome of the last six rolls is 123456. In state 0 you go to state 1 with probability $\frac{1}{6}$ and to state 0 with probability $\frac{5}{6}$, and in state i with $i \leq i \leq 5$, you go to state $i + 1$ with probability $\frac{1}{6}$, to state 1 with probability $\frac{1}{6}$ and to state 0 with probability $\frac{4}{6}$ (how would you simulate from $(\frac{1}{6}, \frac{5}{6})$ and how would you simulate from $(\frac{1}{6}, \frac{1}{6}, \frac{4}{6})$?). The simulation run ends when state 6 is reached or 500 rolls have been done. The desired probability is estimated by dividing the number of simulation runs ending in state 6 by the total number of runs.

5.19. Number the cups as $1, 2, \ldots, 6$. It is no restriction to assume the following procedure. You start with cup 1 and you go from cup i to cup $i + 1$ only after you have correctly guessed the color of the ball in cup i. A key concept in the simulation approach is the concept of state. Let state (i, t, g) mean that you are at cup i with t tokens left and that so far you have already made g wrong guesses for the color of the ball in cup i. You start the process in state $(1, 6, 0)$. The carnival booth owner wins the game if you end up in some state $(i, 0, g)$ and you win the game if you correctly guess the color in some state $(6, t, g)$ with $t \neq 0$. A simulation run goes as follows. Suppose you are in state (i, t, g) with $t \neq 0$. In this state there are $6 - (i - 1) - g = 7 - i - g$ possibilities left for the color of the ball in cup i. A random number u between 0 and 1 is generated. If $u \leq \frac{1}{7-i-g}$ (a correct guess), then the process goes to state $(i + 1, t, 0)$ when $i < 6$ and ends with a win for the player when $i = 6$. If $u > \frac{1}{7-i-g}$ (a wrong guess), then the process goes to state $(i, t-1, g+1)$ if $t > 1$ and ends with a win for the carnival booth if $t = 1$. The win probability of the player is estimated by dividing the number of simulation runs ending in a win for the player by the total number of simulation runs. Subtracting this probability multiplied by 20 from 5 gives an estimate for the average amount won by the carnival booth per game in the long run.

Index